Music and Social Justice

Music and Social Justice

A Guide for Elementary Educators

Cathy Benedict

OXFORD
UNIVERSITY PRESS

OXFORD
UNIVERSITY PRESS

Oxford University Press is a department of the University of Oxford. It furthers
the University's objective of excellence in research, scholarship, and education
by publishing worldwide. Oxford is a registered trade mark of Oxford University
Press in the UK and certain other countries.

Published in the United States of America by Oxford University Press
198 Madison Avenue, New York, NY 10016, United States of America.

Library of Congress Cataloging-in-Publication Data
Names: Benedict, Cathy, author.
Title: Music and social justice : a guide for elementary educators / Cathy Benedict.
Description: New York : Oxford University Press, 2021. |
Includes bibliographical references and index.
Identifiers: LCCN 2020023551 (print) | LCCN 2020023552 (ebook) |
ISBN 9780190062125 (hardback) | ISBN 9780190062132 (paperback) |
ISBN 9780190062156 (epub) | ISBN 9780190062149 (updf) | ISBN 9780190062163 (online)
Subjects: LCSH: Music—Instruction and study—Social aspects. |
Social justice and education. | Education, Elementary.
Classification: LCC MT1.B515 M87 2020 (print) | LCC MT1.B515 (ebook) | DDC 372.87—dc23
LC record available at https://lccn.loc.gov/2020023551
LC ebook record available at https://lccn.loc.gov/2020023552

DOI: 10.1093/oso/9780190062125.001.0001

1 3 5 7 9 8 6 4 2

Paperback printed by Marquis, Canada
Hardback printed by Bridgeport National Bindery, Inc., United States of America

To Patrick

"And I need you more than want you, and I want you for all time."
—Jimmy Webb

Contents

Acknowledgments

As I think through all that made the writing of this book possible, I am reminded immediately of my parents, who never prevented us from bringing any book into the home. I am convinced that whatever lyricism there may be in my writing exists because I was encouraged to read anything and everything. Well, OK, maybe not comic books, but that was a different time, and clearly, I have gotten over that.

Thank you to those who reviewed this manuscript when it was in its infancy. Both your support of my voice and your insight into the directions I should consider helped me believe in the worth of this project.

Thank you to music teacher Laura Meren and her music students in London, Ontario. Over a period of a year Laura allowed me to work with these lessons in her music classes. This book would not be what it is without your help and the access you gave me to your students—in particular, Alex, who I very much hope finds his way in this world.

Thank you to the editors at Oxford University Press. Norm Hirshy, your shepherding first of *The Oxford Handbook of Social Justice in Music Education* followed by this book and whatever contribution it may make to music education in elementary contexts can never be overstated. This would not exist but for you.

Finally, I want to thank Eric Teichman, who, thanks to a generous grant from the music faculty at the University of Western Ontario, helped edit this book from beginning to end. I met Eric when he was an undergraduate at New York University. A fine thinker and pedagogue then and an even more critical and interrogative scholar/teacher now. He knows how I think, knows how I want to think, and, more often than not, directed how I should be thinking. Thank you, Eric, for your keen eye and enduring friendship.

Introduction

During the spring term of 2018, I was asked if I would be willing to welcome groups of fifth-graders enrolled in a gifted program in the local school district for a visit to my university. To the credit of the program, they were visiting not only the university but also other local organizations for students not necessarily university-bound. I am not sure why I took this on; in the moment, it must have seemed like the good-citizen thing to do. Over the course of the day, I met five different groupings of students led by five very different teachers. As the students settled into the class with me, a lot of other "teaching" took place, which meant authoritarian moments of teachers stepping in to intervene on my behalf. This neither surprised nor concerned me. These teachers saw me as a university professor; they couldn't have known that I had taught elementary students for years. No, what caused me distress was the way in which the students had surely been trained to engage with the other.

We had been discussing what one might study in a faculty of music, and the topic of composing for movies came up. One of the young men made an interesting and well-thought-out comment about horror movies without music. Silence, he believed, would not build the same suspense as music would. At that thought, another young man jumped in at the chance to provide examples of movies and even sang recognizable themes. Immediately, one young woman raised her hand and said, "I disagree with that comment; silence can be used just as effectively." I suspect many would have supported her mannered (yet a bit too smug for me) response. In that moment, with hopes of validating the previous comment, I attempted the following: "I am wondering if this is less about disagreeing and agreeing but rather examples of multiple ways of considering how music functions in movies." Nope. Another quick hand in the air, totally dismissing and clearly disagreeing with me: "I agree with Alison's comment." Again, a bit too smug, considering that it now felt as if gender lines were being drawn. After one more attempt to move discussion past agreeing and disagreeing, I recognized (remarkably) that in the time I had with them, I did not stand a chance against these young women and their formidable wall of what counts as discussion.

Music and Social Justice. Cathy Benedict, Oxford University Press (2021). © Oxford University Press.
DOI: 10.1093/oso/9780190062125.003.0001.

My use of the word *smug* here may feel facetious, but after those two young women cleared the space for their disagreement to be heard (the raising of the hand), they stopped listening to anything that followed. Granted, the comment that silence is powerful implied a level of listening, but it was presented as proof of accomplished thinking skills rather than as a considered encounter with another's thinking "where the question of meaning arises" (Vansieleghem, 2005, p. 32). I, of course, would have loved something like the following: "Gosh, I've heard those moments, too, but now I am remembering times when silence is used in scary ways!" This, in my imagined world, would be followed by more laugher, more singing of movie, television and video themes and outright, spontaneous joy.

I imagine that most people observing the classes would have been impressed with these responses, always prefaced with the obligatory hand in the air. But for me, it felt more like an obedient display of consideration cloaked in false generosity. If these students can be trained to raise their hands and preface remarks with particular phrases, they can absolutely be encouraged to talk through what quickly raising hands does to the thinking spaces of others. They can also grapple with the problematics of simply agreeing and disagreeing. We only have to learn how to take time and scaffold those discussions. Clearly, I should have been more prepared for the "agree and disagree" framing of what constitutes discussion. After all, this is what first-year university students perceive equitable listening to be; they had to have learned this skill somewhere.

But what is equitable? What is listening? What *is* the purpose of meeting the other?

It may seem odd to begin a book that ostensibly sets out to address social justice with a scenario depicting the epistemological fireworks of privileged students labeled as gifted. But this is exactly where we should begin, for where does social justice begin? Social justice for whom?

In the following pages, I address these questions and others that will emerge as I pursue ways to approach and present a framework for enacting socially just engagements. First and foremost, social justice is not something outside of us, something we can give or provide to others. There is no one way to teach "social justice." Even the question "How do I teach social justice?" suggests a thing that can be planned, implemented, and assessed. Far more complicated than that, and even antithetical to the goal of challenging systems that reproduce inequities, teaching can't be a series of steps leading toward a predetermined end of enlightenment. Life is far too multitudinous to carry such a definition of success, the burden far too prohibitive. Fraught with failure, one can't expect spaces of kindness and generosity to present themselves in every lived moment. Yet it is exactly this impossibility that makes the possible so wondrous.

As I hope to demonstrate in following chapters, assuming pedagogical dispositions that shift and disrupt and a way of being with others that embraces complexities—perhaps even a bit of (organized) bedlam—doesn't have to be daunting. The goal is to find comfort and certainty in spaces that don't immediately (and may never) present themselves as settled or controlled, even at the elementary level. Especially at the elementary level.

How to "Read" the Book

The book is composed of a series of chapters that present scenarios, unit ideas, and lesson-plan templates that both challenge and reframe traditional ways of "dealing with" many of the topics we have come to think of as social justice. Thus, rather than present lists, sequences, or learning hierarchies on which to build, I will continue to return to the most essential and powerful disposition we must take on: care with the words we use, in all moments. Words, dialogue, wonderment, and curiosities, however, all need a context. Accordingly, then, some of the chapters are anchored by texts (both musical and written), enduring and essential questions, others by musicking engagements, and others by persisting political and philosophically wicked problems, or those issues that by their very nature will always bear resistance to determined solutions.

Throughout the book, I also include examples of dialogue taken from data collected in a research project I conducted at an elementary (kindergarten–eighth grade) school in London, Ontario, during the 2018–2019 school year. I am forever grateful to their music teacher, Laura Meren, and to the students, who did not have any reason to trust me other than that their beloved music teacher asked them to do so. I learned several things during my time at their school. It was far more challenging to ask the younger ones to speak with one another (although with practice they were able to take this on), but they often had fewer cares about speaking out loud and sharing with the class. With the sixth–eighth grades, it was almost impossible to get them all to speak, let alone speak with the other. They did not know me, and that went a long way in explaining their reluctance, but it didn't explain a narrative I found particularly troubling when it comes to a desire to foster plurality in the classroom. I want to be very mindful as I think this next point through. We now live in a world that more readily recognizes injustice. Students are more able to speak up when they feel an injustice has occurred, so much so that they are very capable of wielding that discourse to their advantage. Let me explain what I mean. When I bring up issues such as race, when I engage in dialogue that calls attention to the problematics of color-blind and religion-blind practices, students are more apt to call out (for instance), "Teacher! That's racist!" before I can even broach a conversation with them. I would imagine that this kind of reaction from students prevents teachers from moving forward with conversations that might challenge and interrogate this kind of response, particularly when these responses come fast and furious. But it must be done.

I also met a new response that I found particularly troubling and one that is even more impossible to interrogate. I have taught students of all ages for a long time, and I believe I have a sense of when a student is using something as an excuse to not engage, so I take great care here as I make this next point. For the first time, I watched as students said, "I don't feel comfortable sharing," in contexts that had little or nothing to do with self-revealing, other than their thinking on an issue. Here is the thing: I respect this, I honor this ability to recognize one's points of care, but I witnessed something quite like the "That's racist" comment, where after the statement was delivered, any point of conversation came to a halt. This is not a "good" thing. Our challenge is to create spaces where students can talk through these responses and others like them. Of course, I have not witnessed this kind of response in classes where I have had the opportunity of time and trust, but it rang a warning bell to me. The implications are worrisome if our goal is to create spaces in which plurality and all ways of knowing and being can be honored. What I learned during these moments is that in this context, students desperately needed help in learning how to speak and listen with the other. This had nothing to do with their music teacher, who was kind, caring, generous, and musical at all times. It had everything to do with the general educative ethos that pervades schooling, which values individual accountability above all else.

By no means is this a comprehensive curriculum guide. The chapters are presented in such a way as to suggest depth of pedagogical engagement that can then be transferred to other contexts. The goal is to open spaces for students to, as Paulo Freire (1970) would say, "[reflect] and [act] upon the world in order to transform it" (p. 33), by providing the opportunity for students to question what is perceived as objective reality. This is not a developmental issue. Scaffolding ways of knowing and interacting with the world can be presented from the very beginning through the language we use from prekindergarten forward. Music educators often have the gift of constancy and consistency with their students, meeting them in kindergarten or at the beginning of high school and then sending them on their way sometimes years later. Why not model interrogative language that provides a differing "sort of permanent disposition of action toward the world" (Dewey, 1964, p. 325)? Thinking and contemplative strategies that ask students to question what they *think* they know and how they *came* to know is only one example of a permanent disposition that embraces wonderment rather than certainty. Hence, continually returning to multiple ways of what it means to know frames the chapters.

In chapter 1, I briefly address my own background and the experiences and musical "training" that brought me to this current place of thinking and writing. At the heart of chapter 1 is the message that frames the rest of the book: our relationships with others are what matter most. At the heart of socially just encounters, then, is the ability to listen and respond to the other—not what we think the other will say, not what we predict the other will say, but to listen in the moment. This kind of genuine dialogue (Buber, 1947/2002) is not something we normally experience, particularly in schools. I delineate exactly what is meant by that as I provide examples of what dialogue is not and what it can be.

Chapter 2 extends the dialogue model from chapter 1 to a practical example of thinking through the term *communication*. With the goal of teaching students how to ask different kinds of questions that help to uncover misinformation and bias—that help the other think more deeply—I outline a thinking-map exercise appropriate for all ages, elementary through university students. I then situate lullaby as a form of communication rather than simply as something one does or learns. The goal here is to introduce and present opportunities for genuine dialogue that might not occur otherwise, particularly at a very young age. Thus, I introduce texts that help students wonder: Who gets to sing a lullaby? How do certain interpretations come to be shaped and normalized, and what does that mean for those who hear and understand relationships differently? Indeed, is there an essential property of lullaby? When is a lullaby not a lullaby, and who gets to decide?

Through a series of scaffolded lesson plans that begin innocuously enough, chapter 3 addresses friendship and bullying. I use the word *innocuously* because in a world in which children of all ages are confronted by public language that is less than respectful—indeed, where world leaders such as Donald Trump model language such as "moron, lowlife, loose, *the* African Americans, *the* blacks, *the* Latinos, *the* women" (Andersen, 2018, emphasis added)—very little is innocuous anymore. Bullying has always lived on the world stage, always in society-made disenfranchisement, always in conflict, always in war. We dialogue with students, "loving, humble, and full of faith," so that all of us may move "into ever closer partnership in the naming of the world" (Freire, 2000, p. 91). The texts used in this chapter begin "small" enough but move quickly into texts (including a movie version of *Peter and the Wolf*) that push students to consider systemic poverty and war as forms of bullying.

Creating, manipulating, organizing, mixing, and remixing sounds can offer an artistic endeavor that supports opportunities for students in all grades to speak through sound and promote social awareness and dialogue. Soundscapes are one such practice that can engage students in both the compositional process and critical exploration of their world and the worlds of others. Chapter 4, written in conversation with Kelly Bylica, presents a unit documenting a soundscape project that can be implemented with students of all ages.

We live in a time in which fluid movement brought on by conflicts, war, and general injustices has brought to our attention the ways in which spiritual and religious beliefs, ways of knowing and being in the world, are positioned as conflicting and radically incompatible. Hardly a comprehensive guide to an in-depth understanding of these ways of knowing the world, chapter 5 aims to lay out a rationale for what happens when we engage in religion-blind practices, as well as to present general lesson ideas and examples of dialogue that help all of us consider how we come to know our world through belief and unbelief systems.

Music has always been intertwined with social movements. People use songs, and they are mediated by songs. Music shapes society, and society is shaped by music and musicking. Elementary students are more than able to grapple with concepts such as identity construction and representation in song. Music as protest, propaganda, and resistance (Street, 2017) is also well within their cognitive, if not visceral, understanding. Chapter 6 serves to remind us that listening to and performing music can lead toward the heightened awareness of social inequities—but that this does not happen magically. With the help of John Lennon and Sly and the Family Stone, I think through the ways in which music gets used the way it is used, as well as what happens to musics that were intended for a *socially driven purpose* but become used in ways that undermine their original social significance?

Chapter 7 places all these ideas in the context of policy and presents a new way of looking at policy as intrinsically connected to the work of teachers. Patrick Schmidt helps the teacher see the differences between policy as a daily practice in the school and community context and policies as rules and regulations organized around policy texts. He thus offers a vision that links policy to pedagogical process, articulating this in terms of conscientization, participation, and activism.

The book then closes with a brief afterword, where I reflect on the place of dialogue in the social and the musical. Returning always to John Dewey as we think through listening that challenges and moves beyond one-way engagements, I think back upon moments that both forced and allowed me to be and do differently.

Can elementary students (first–eighth grade) encounter the other and imagine differently what that encounter may bring to who they are? Can they give up the certainty of "knowing"? I *know* that they can, and I *know* that they want to. Daniel and Auriac (2011) remind us that "complex thinking is neither innate nor magic" (p. 241); it is not something to which we are born, and it doesn't magically appear when we turn a certain age. If we are to imagine a world in which our relationships with the other bear witness to care/interest, generosity/courage, then moments rather than movements, the now rather than progress, must guide our engagements. It may feel impossible—that everything works against what I am going to suggest—but it is exactly that impossibility that makes life in and through music education so deliriously possible.

1

Listening and Responding

Dialogue in Practice

As a slogan, you can't beat *social justice*. It's ambiguous, and it can be wielded by anyone, making it almost impossible to interrogate and making its purpose up for grabs. The phrase covers intent and interest, while at the same time causing users to feel really good about themselves for using it. I have come to believe that it is rather naive to suppose social justice as an end goal, or even an aim. It is not the concept on which I have given up but rather the concept of goal as something patiently worked toward and finally realized. I recognize there are implications for giving up on this goal, not simply the repercussions of giving up on our objective reality but those of giving up on our ethical obligations. However, I'm not sure I even know what social justice means. I'm not convinced I need to, though, because I am wondering lately if worrying about what it means might actually prevent us from, as Maxine Greene (2007) writes, "moving beyond the abstract to the concrete" (p. 1).

Where does social justice reside? Perhaps it comes down to not focusing on social justice or socially just actions but "simply" (!) the space I inhabit with others. And more particularly, those students who come through my door. Surely, I can "empower" them to enact social justice in the very small space and very short time we share together?

Woven throughout every chapter in this book is the conviction that our relationships with others are what matter most. It is not transformational change that should be guiding our decisions but rather the moment of the interaction, the responsive reaction of uncovering with another. Each time we meet the other with predisposed ideas, biases, and assumptions, we shut down possibilities for ourselves and possibilities for the world. How we go about knowing the other opens up how we come to know ourselves.

Thus, in this chapter, I present and interrogate pedagogical engagements that have traditionally been viewed as ways to structure democracy—equity and fairness—in classrooms. I grapple with how and to what end hyper-individualism has permeated our educative spaces. I trouble the current favorite discourse of empowerment and question the rhetorical force this has

Music and Social Justice. Cathy Benedict, Oxford University Press (2021). © Oxford University Press.
DOI: 10.1093/oso/9780190062125.003.0002.

taken on. I present the groundwork for engendering epistemic humility or, in other words, the groundwork for honoring multiple ways of knowing.

We need to learn how to listen better than we do, to music, to the world around us, even to ourselves. But more than anything, we need to learn how to listen and respond to the other. We live together in this world, and as Hannah Arendt (1958) writes, we "experience meaningfulness only because [we] can talk with and make sense to each other and to [ourselves]" (p. 4). In other words, it is only because we live among others that we are able to find meaning. Alone, and this can also mean living surrounded by only those who are "like" us, we are unable to engage with difference and experience distinction. Thus, at the heart of the socially just human is being able to listen and respond to the other. Consequently, questions such as "Who am I?" "How have I come to be?" and "How do my actions with others encourage or prohibit engagements of inclusivity?" not only underscore this opening chapter but serve as guiding ethical ideals for each subsequent chapter.

Toward Listening and Responding

My path toward this moment in time was forged by several experiences, not least among those my more than 15 years teaching elementary music. Perhaps like many music teachers, I realized after graduating with my teaching credentials that I didn't really know *how* to teach elementary music. I had a few ideas and some songs I could teach but no real pedagogical strategies. I had spent the previous three summers working on my Orff certification, so I had a sense of possible creative encounters, but nothing felt concrete. After one year of teaching, I took a year off to study for a master's degree at Holy Names University and receive my Kodály certification. During that time, I was not only immersed in Kodály methodology, but I was also going into a first-grade class once a week to teach what I was studying. It was a remarkable experience and one, it is safe to say, that transformed my teaching and how I saw myself as a teacher. For the next 15 years, I was intent on teaching literacy. Of course, at that time, literacy meant only one thing to me: how to read and write Western classical notation. Conceptions of critical literacy were not to come until much later, as I began my doctoral studies in curriculum and teaching. During that time, however, Kodály sequencing provided a direct and uncomplicated way forward. By the time my students (and I did indeed think of the students as "mine") graduated from fifth grade, they were performing three-part Kodály and Bartók choral works, making me look very good. And I held that power completely, all the way through my first year of doctoral studies—which I had begun in order to teach others how to teach music or, rather, how to teach Kodály.

I look back over those years and now am able to think of my notion of literacy then as functional. I am fairly certain I have used this Gutstein (2006) quote a million times, but he frames functional literacy in such a way that it is worth citing him over and over: "a literacy is functional when it serves the productive purposes (i.e., maintaining the status quo) of the dominant interests in society" (p. 5). What an indictment this citation is in the context of my use! And yet I stand by it and its relationship to how and why I was teaching the way I was. The students in front of me, "my" students, were there to serve me, to serve the reproduction of Western classical texts. They were there to learn to read "music" more as a cocktail-party skill than as anything they would take into their lives in any meaningful, lifelong way.

I am not saying that what they learned wasn't musical, nor did I do any real harm. But I did forsake the person in front of me, the human in front of me, in order to further my musical agenda. The brilliance of Kodály sequencing is that if one follows the suggested script, students are led toward the uncovering of "literacy." The teacher asks a series of questions and moves forward to the ultimate already known, the naming of the musical element. I believed in the openness and generosity of the questions I was asking until I began audio recording my fifth-grade classes for an assignment in one of my doctoral classes. As I transcribed those recordings, I realized that what I had believed was thoughtful student input (never discussion; even at the time, I didn't pretend there was discussion) was simply the same students answering the questions I was posing. The words of Vivian Gussin Paley (1986) hit me hard:

> The tape recorder, with its unrelenting fidelity, captured the unheard or unfished murmur, the misunderstood and mystifying context, the disembodied voices asking for clarification and comfort. It also captured the impatience in *my* voice as children struggled for attention, approval, and justice. (p. 123)

In my case, there was always one correct answer. *What note equals do?* "G." *Where does it live?* "On the second line." If a student responded, "The fourth line," my retort was a negative. It wasn't until much later, when I was able to confront my own voice, that I learned to ask students how they figured that out—realizing that the answer "the fourth line" indicated evidence of reasoning in the students' thinking. They were simply counting from the "wrong" direction! That one seemingly simple shift changed my path forever. From that moment on, when I asked a question and received a response, I began asking: *How did you figure that out? Tell me more about your thinking. Talk out loud about your processing. Take me to new places, to places that help me see my own thinking differently, places that help me better know who I am.*

What Kind of Dialogue? For What Purpose?

For a very long time, I believed that if I only modeled the process of listening and responding, students would intuitively pick up on that and do the same. Teachers, after all, wield a lot of power. Students learn from a very early age what the teacher wants: the correct response, the teacher response. They know because these are the kinds of answers teachers often respond to and actively look for. They also learn not to bother if they don't have what they know to be the "right" answer. It takes only one arched eyebrow to learn that keeping to oneself staves off, at best, disappointment and, at worst, humiliation. Someone else always has the right answer, and since teachers are more often than not content with the first right answer we receive, we too often close off other possibilities, other ways of seeing the answer. When we do call on the students who appear to need support, at the first sign of hesitation, we swoop in to finish the answer for them. All we need is a sign that indicates superficial understanding, and we assume (hope for) understanding. This kind of hope, however, does little to further the thinking of the student. It is a blind kind of hopeful hope, in which the present moment of growth is sacrificed for a future that promises the (magical) appearance and formation of voice. This is not the hope of Paulo Freire (1994) that is "rooted in practice, in the struggle" (p. 8). While it may seem supportive, in all actuality, students learn quite quickly that they will be "saved" from having to engage in the learning process—a learning process they have come to see as one that doesn't deserve or support their engagement.

I always have conversations with the university students in the classes I teach who are on the path to teacher licensure about why we accept the first right answer and why we shy away from what we perceive to be intellectual struggle. The second question makes more sense to them, as they recognize an element of care in not wanting struggling students to fail. We finish sentences of students because we want them to feel supported; we want to save them from failure. Discussion around the first question about why we look for the right answer opens up reflexive spaces that can lead toward issues of control, knowing better, dominance, reproduction. These are never easy or simple discussions, yet they are necessary if we seek to interrogate a world that rarely, if ever, embraces everyone equally.

Just as students deserve to be taught how to read texts critically, as many curriculum and policy documents ask of teachers, so, too, do they deserve to be taught how to listen and respond in ways that open up spaces for new ways of knowing themselves and the other. Unfortunately, these policy documents are almost always linked to career readiness and competition in the global market. I use the word *unfortunately* purposely in this context, as competition in the market demands the preparation of hyper-individuality, too often at the expense of the development of community and plurality. Yet plurality is at the heart of socially just engagements; it is who we are. To ignore plurality is to deny who we are as distinct individuals (Arendt, 1958); it is to deny this world of multifaceted and multitudinous individuals who must, in our responsibility to the world, find a way to live together. It is to deny the child/student/human in front of us.

Even very young students can tell you what it means to be seen and known, to be listened to and responded to. Unfortunately, we experience this so seldom. And it begins when we are very young. I can't count the number of times I have attempted to have conversations with the young children in our neighborhood and the caregiver/parent steps in to answer the simplest of questions I have posed. These conversations tend to go something like this:

CATHY: (my eyes locked on Christopher) Hi, Christopher! Tell me what you're doing with that shovel.

CHRISTOPHER: Well, ummm . . .

CAREGIVER: Oh, Chris is digging up worms.

CATHY: (my eyes not wavering from Christopher's) Worms, eh, Christopher? What do you want to do with them?

CHRISTOPHER: Well, ummm . . .

CAREGIVER: He is planning to take them to school.

CATHY: (eyes still on Christopher) School, huh? What are you going to do with them at school, Christopher? (I figure if I keep using his name, the adult will figure out I really am speaking to Christopher and not to them.)

CHRISTOPHER: Well, I really . . . (At this juncture, before Christopher can really say anything, the adult shepherds Christopher from the scene, worried that he has made a nuisance of himself.)

The point here is that it's not just teachers who answer for children. Way before children end up in the formal confines of schooling, other adults are stepping in to speak for them. And yet we expect children to become independent learners, equipped to succeed in college and career, able to work collaboratively and respond to those around them. So much of what we do works against this. We place them in small groups, and then we hover over them, checking in on them to see if everyone is "on task." We have been conditioned not to trust that they can discuss together without us. Indeed, they have not been taught how to discuss together beyond getting the task done through designated roles. The task is already known, the rubric already assigned, the format of the response dictated by the constraints of the five-paragraph essay. Accountability is always omnipresent. We use the other for predetermined ends.

Martin Buber, theologian and philosopher, spent much of his life considering the importance of dialogue and made a distinction among three kinds. Technical dialogue, where "the focal point of the exchange" is to "understand something, or gain information" (Kramer & Gawlick, 2003, p. 33), has a concrete importance in the daily lives of students when not framed or presented as the only purpose of dialogue. Unfortunately, this kind of dialogue lends itself to assessment and accountability and is one that permeates not just practical engagements but social ones as well. Perhaps more distressing, however, is "monologue disguised as dialogue" (Buber, 1947/2002, p. 22), one that so often underlies the "I agree" or "I disagree" engagements that students are often trained to undertake. These kinds of discussion techniques are ostensibly geared toward teaching students how to respond to the comments of others. Strategies, or rules of engagement, such as affirming the speaker and then following up with choosing to elaborate on what the previous speaker said, making connections to your own thinking or even diverging and redirecting the conversation, are all effective ways of helping students navigate small- and large-group discussions. While researchers such as Stephen Brookfield and Stephen Preskill (1999) suggest that one such follow-up technique in a discussion is to ask furthering questions of the speaker, this strategy, too, deserves more careful attention.

Here is my thinking about this issue of class discussion techniques, one that moves us closer to Buber's third kind (1947/2002), "genuine dialogue" (p. 22). Yes, students need to be taught how to engage in discussions. This has to be modeled and explicitly referenced, but I want to look more closely at these techniques and what values they may be underscoring. First of all, when we teach techniques such as those above, students begin to see them as formulaic, much like the two students from the introduction who knew they were supposed to acknowledge/affirm the speaker before moving on to agreeing or disagreeing. But what does it mean to affirm the speaker, even to empower the speaker? Yes, we may remark that we really like what the person is saying, we may even share that their comments help us see our own thinking in a new way, so the speaker knows at the very least that we were listening on some level, but is this affirmation? Well, yes and no. Yes, in that affirmation more often than not looks like this as we talk back and forth at each other, as we exchange words. If our goal is to be present to the other so that in this presence,

I come to know the possibilities of myself through and with the other, however, then the simple exchange of words will not establish, as Buber (1947/2002) writes, "a living mutual relation" (p. 22). Being with others in ways that acknowledge the person in front of us beyond superficial affirmation is what Maurice Friedman calls an "ethical ought" (quoted in Buber, 1947/2003). We need to learn how to meet the other "with no preparation other than my readiness to respond with my whole being to the unforeseen and the unique" (p. xvi). This is, of course, easier said than practiced. And it calls for each of us to suspend what we perceive to be our own immediate needs; it is to move beyond an affirmation of one's own individual success and "the desire to have one's own self-reliance confirmed" (Buber, 1947/2003, p. 23).

This also means re-evaluating what is meant by the word *empowerment*, as the term is often used to suggest the growth of self-reliance or independence. *Empowerment* has entered our everyday discourse to such an extent we no longer think of what it means. We are empowered to act, change, speak back, learn, be diverse, purchase the "right" thing; you name it, we have been empowered to do it. However, we ought to note that this ambiguity can serve to "[obscure] different and possible social interests" (Popkewitz, 1980, p. 4). In other words, when we are empowered to buy something, we may forget that we don't have to buy that something and that the word has been co-opted by a very particular interest and is being used quite possibly without our best intentions in mind. Corporations can't empower us. Outside forces can't empower us. This, of course, means we cannot empower others, not even our students. Our students are only empowered when they come to recognize the ways in which these forces act upon them and they then "act to change the conditions of their life" (Bookman & Morgen, 1988, p. 4).

Moving toward genuine dialogue also means revisiting the purpose of raising hands so that the teacher might decide and control who speaks. I have been in many classrooms throughout the world, and I have made it a habit to take photos of the seemingly universal tradition of posting classroom rules on the wall. Inevitably, no matter the country or language, the rules center around keeping one's hands and feet to oneself, respecting others, raising hands, and not speaking until called upon. In a research project I did with colleagues in Greece, Finland, and Sweden, we found that students in all of our contexts understood two things to be very clear:

1. Even when asked to make the rules up themselves, they know what the teacher wants included on the list.
2. They also know that all of these rules are negotiable, particularly if the teacher likes you.

It seems rather remarkable and almost impossible to ask students to think differently when they recognize the problematics of the official world and are keenly aware of the hidden one. Providing the space so they can articulate how the world works on them and to them is one way to open up stories told together as "a means of sense making, a way in and through which we represent, interrogate, and interpret experience and come to know ourselves and [each other]" (Barrett & Stauffer, 2012, p. 1).

When I taught in New York City, I often would note that even the very young students knew whose electricity came back on first during a power outage. Each of the chapters in this book serves as a way to provide the space for students to tell the stories of injustice. But telling stories isn't enough. Barrett and Stauffer also remind us that as teachers, we need to find ways to help all of our students interrogate these stories: how did this come to be, how does my behavior either forward or prevent injustices, what action can we take together to be different in this world?

We aren't really taught how to engage in this kind of critical dialogue. We are taught that respectful agreeing or disagreeing with someone demonstrates attention to the other. But too often, agreeing or disagreeing is simply a polite mechanism we use to cover the fact that we already know what we are going to say. Agreeing and disagreeing are wielded as strategies that suggest the appearance of listening. Of course, to some extent, there is listening, but what kind of listening and for what purpose are woefully unarticulated.

In the next section, I provide examples of how I go about modeling this process with both university students and elementary students. Note that these strategies, much like anything new we introduce that challenges how things have always been done, will not go the way you hope they will go the first few times or even perhaps the millionth time you attempt them. However, not going the way one hopes is completely different from framing this as a process that either works or doesn't work. What we try always works. We can just never be sure of what, at what, and to what end it works. This is an important distinction when we think of "methods" that work and are linked to teacher control and student subservience. Yes, the methods we used worked to "get them" to play in tune, but what is left in their wake? What other possibilities are missed? Thus, thinking of these strategies as processes that continue to develop throughout our lives is important to continually underscore with students.

Listening and Responding: Dialogue in Practice

As I wrote above, I am now at the point of my teaching where I recognize the importance of articulating my thinking and reasoning. I no longer assume students will "pick up" on my modeling. I have conversations, even meta-think-out-loud conversations, with students about why I am making the choices I am making. Thus, I often begin this task by modeling what discussion is *not*.

The moment first presents itself after any kind of discussion has taken place— so almost immediately and always during our initial class encounter. I stop the class and tell them that I want us all to work on responding to the other in ways that might be new for us. I ask for a volunteer and say that I am going to model the possibilities of what that looks like. I place myself in front of the student and ask a question that can come directly from the discussion we were having previous to this moment or anything I know will instigate a response.

CATHY: Hey, Morgan, what made you decide to become a music teacher?

MORGAN: My music teacher in high school was really cool and supportive and—

CATHY: Hey, mine was, too! He really encouraged us all to come in at lunch and hang out. He had us playing all kinds of music that everyone just loved.

MORGAN: Yeah, everyone loved the music we were playing, too, and the contests we went to were—

CATHY: Oh, gosh! We went to contests as well. I really loved those. I always had a great time!

MORGAN: I guess I did as well, but we really had to work hard and long on the music we were going to perform and sometimes—

CATHY: But that was the best part for me! I loved playing the same music over and over till everyone could finally play their parts. Thanks, Morgan! It was great to remember why I went into teaching!

When I ask the "Morgan" of the moment how the conversation felt, they always share that they felt ignored and dismissed, that they had no voice. But theoretically, I was affirming the points Morgan was making; I responded to everything she raised. I note that I interrupted because I was so excited to think about and share with Morgan my own experience, a common occurrence when we exchange with others. But this conversation was really about me, or I made it about me, or I was unable to make it about Morgan.

All of these issues and more emerge as we reflect on this demonstration. Both Morgan and the other students in the class recognize the falseness of the exchange, while realizing this is reflective of most of the discussions they have with others.

I then begin again with Morgan, using the same questions.

CATHY: Hey, Morgan, what made you decide to become a music teacher?

MORGAN: My music teacher in high school was really cool and supportive and . . . (Morgan's response tapers off into silence)

CATHY: Tell me more about what you mean by supportive.

MORGAN: Well, she encouraged us to join her at lunch every day, and that felt good.

CATHY]: What felt good about that?

MORGAN: I'm not sure; it just did.

CATHY: I wonder how the others felt when you met up at lunch.

MORGAN: Oh, we had a great time! Sometimes we would work on the music or just talk. It didn't matter.

CATHY: Why do you say it didn't matter?

This is a completely different encounter. As the listener and responder, I must be in the moment with Morgan. I can't assume I know what Morgan will say, nor can I have a list of responses ready to go. If my "ethical ought" is to respond to the person in the moment, I especially can't bring her points back to myself. Of course, I want to share my own experiences, I want Morgan to know that what she said speaks to my own experiences, but at this moment in time, I want to be with Morgan. I want to experience surprise and wonder and think anew.

I then pair students up and make them practice this exercise, taking a full five-minute turn at each role. I time this, as it is difficult to sustain this kind of discussion. They often want to give up and switch over before their time is up. After they do this, I ask them to write down how they felt as they took on each role. I didn't always do this, because I assumed they would all love how it felt to be heard and responded to. It turns out, however, that some express feeling interrogated and that their responses aren't good enough. Of course, this can be because their partner, having never experienced this kind of responding, took on a kind of cross-examining stance. But it could also be that, having never really been responded to in such a way, they felt threatened and, indeed, not good enough. Why shouldn't the ways they responded to their partner's inquiries be enough, when it always had been in the past?

Needless to say, we have to keep returning to this kind of listening and responding multiple times throughout the semester. In fact, just when I think it has become the class norm, a student will say something like, "Oh, I thought you just wanted us to write down what they were saying!" This is often followed by laughter and lighthearted comments such as, "You know by now what she wants!" I choose to think of these as lighthearted because it *is* my expectation. Just as we can reward every hand that flies up into the air with the "answer," we can just as easily "reward" this kind of dialogue. I have also seen, however, this kind of responding tip over into what does indeed feel like interrogation. Indeed, I once watched Morgan in class become more aggressive with her response, because she was intent on "helping" her partner question an assumption she was making. As I watched the other student begin to wither, I stepped in (probably not as calmly as I would have liked) to stop the process. Later on, I spoke with Morgan, and we talked through what had happened in that moment. She recognized that the student was not ready to move deeper into her own thinking on the topic. Clearly, moments such as these will always be part of this kind of dialogue, but surely this should not prevent us from an "ethical ought." Just as we talk through what this kind of dialogue means, we also need to talk through with our students the moments that begin to feel like interrogation rather than genuine dialogue.

This is not a skill that belongs or even begins only at the high school or university level. At the university level, this process looks different, as the students have come from contexts in high school where discussion was more prevalent than it might be at the elementary level. However, the sooner we begin modeling this kind of expectation, the easier it is for these kinds of dispositions to become the norm. At the elementary/middle-school level, this is more challenging for several reasons. Before high school, with its dispersed groupings that begin based on differentiation of interest and, more unfortunately, ability, students at the elementary level are for the most part grouped into a mass of diversity and plurality. While these points can also be directed at upper-level groups, teachers at the elementary level may shy away from scaffolding this kind of discussion, because they are concerned about order (classroom management), turn taking (raising hands), control (if there is no discussion, students won't be able to express controversial ideas), and the clash of incommensurable ideas. When we teach this way, however, we might as well be saying, "If I ignore the people in front of me (whether that means engaging in color-blind or even religion-blind practices), we can all just get along."

One way to begin this kind of demonstration is to assign, even with very young students, an interview project based on, for instance, one's favorite kind of music. These kinds of projects are powerful, in that the people being interviewed often feel grateful to be asked about their thinking, particularly when these assignments are geared toward intergenerational exchanges. Teachers, however, have to be cognizant of framing this kind of assignment as asking another adult, rather than "going home" and "asking one's parents." There may not be a home or parents.

I often grab the beloved secretary or custodian and interview them in front of the students. I ask the students to take notes on how I interact and respond to the person as well as the *kinds* of questions I ask. You can use a chart for younger ones, opening up the conversation previous to the interview by asking the class what makes a thoughtful and caring interview. It is also helpful in this context to demonstrate the same kind of encounter I had with

Morgan. Students can compare the different styles, with the goal of moving away from questions that can be answered with short yes-or-no responses toward helping the interviewees think more deeply about their responses.

When I present this to my own university students or at workshops, I am almost always asked at what age one can begin doing this with students. My first response is always to point out that the question suggests that there is an optimal "developmentally appropriate time" to begin, that we have been taught that young students are unable to encounter the other in this way. Indeed, this may be true with very young ones, but this doesn't mean we should not try to continually return to what it means to hear and come to know the other. Even throughout my teaching career at the university level, I have continued to work this way in classrooms with young students of all ages. While teachers have expectations that students will become independent learners and musicians, I have come to realize that we don't teach students how to do this, neither through dialogue nor through musicking. The worry or concern that one doesn't have time to teach students how to listen and how to care for the other only serves to alienate our students further from socially just engagements. Here is the thing: these spaces do not always appear, as Arendt would remind us, but to be deprived of them and to deprive others of them is to deny each of us the possibility of plurality. It is not just to be blind to the other but to deny the other.

We would do well to remind ourselves that not every student loves mathematics. Why should music be any different? The point here is not the subject but the student, the relational. Nel Noddings (2003), living her life as a mathematician, educator, and philosopher, reminds us of this throughout her work:

> Among the intangibles that I would have my students carry away is the feeling that the subject we have struggled with is both fascinating and boring, significant and silly, fraught with meaning and nonsense, challenging and tedious, and that whatever attitude we take toward it, it will not diminish our regard for each other. The student is infinitely more important than the subject. (p. 29)

In the following chapters, I present examples of lesson plans, ranging from the elementary- to the middle-school classroom (and many of those plans can be extended into high school), that reflect both the importance of the subject (in our case, music) and the infinite importance of the relational.

A note, however, on how I view lesson planning bears stating. I recognize that many administrators and teachers focus on classroom management. This is not a phrase I use, as "managing" another human suggests relationships that are governed and controlled by the teacher. I do, however, recognize the importance of the creation of a safe space. Many of the lessons I present can be used in such a way that they can take up the entire class period. On the other hand, many of the concepts can and should be embedded throughout the flow of several lessons. In those cases, I articulate what that might look like.

The point I want to make is twofold. First, a well-crafted lesson with tight musical transitions between each musical encounter not only keeps the attention of the students but also keeps them busy musically, thus serving to diminish the time-honored tradition of pushing the boundaries of both the class and the teacher. Second, a well-crafted lesson that is grounded on principles of the relational and socially just engagements ought not to be seen as something out of reach and actually might go a long way toward mitigating and negating the need to push boundaries in order to be seen and heard. Berger (2007) reminds us that "the promise of a movement is its future victory; whereas the promises of the incidental moments are instantaneous" (p. 8). As music teachers, we often have the luxury of continuity over the years with students. Imagine the potential in shifting our focus from the promise of some future victory to the immediate, infinite possibilities of incidental moments.

2

Communicating Justice and Equity

Meeting the Other

Embedded in most music education curricula is the idea that music has long been a way to communicate. Game songs are found in cultures throughout the world; children play passing games, chanting games, hand games, all seemingly connecting with others through music. Music through song is used to communicate care, love, honor, and respect. Music through song is also used to communicate anger, hatred, bigotry and racism. *But what does it mean to communicate? Who gets to communicate? Is expression without reciprocity communication? What, then, is the purpose of communication and its relationship to equity and socially just actions? How does this relationship manifest in music education?*

I place these particular questions in this chapter for much the same reason I outline in chapter 1 how to go about teaching genuine dialogue. As music educators, we have plenty of models for curriculum development. In the United States, music educators have access to the Common Core State Standards as well as the National Core Arts Standards. Beyond that, many states and districts have their own curriculum documents. In Canada, much like in the United States, each province has a curriculum guide outlining both scope and sequence. Clearly, there is no lack of curriculum models to which music educators might refer. I often joke with preservice students that because of their intense musical training, they already possess many musical skills that might lend themselves toward "teaching music." As preservice music educators, then, fitting what might already be "known" into those curriculum documents hardly seems a challenge. Many of them experienced repertoire as curriculum, and most, if not all, experienced curriculum as teaching/learning music literacy. But the skills they usually don't have are those with which to interrogate the models they came from, which means addressing the equity of who may have benefited from those curriculum models and who quite possibility did not. What just might be needed, then, is a more holistic view of engaging with both the human and the musicking context in such a way that relationships with the other remain at the center.

Many of those national and state/provincial curriculum documents are anchored by both enduring understandings and essential questions, so as to,

Music and Social Justice. Cathy Benedict, Oxford University Press (2021). © Oxford University Press.
DOI: 10.1093/oso/9780190062125.003.0003.

for instance, "organize the information, skills and experiences within artistic processes" (National Coalition for Core Arts Standards, 2014, p. 1). Beyond focusing solely on artistic processes, however, broad, open-ended questions that anchor the growth of musicianship to larger conceptual issues are absolutely one way to help keep plurality and the relational at the forefront. The endless possibilities of formulating questions that lead one further and further into how one comes to know the world quite nicely translate into possible units within the larger scope of a music curriculum.

I am convinced that even young students (indeed, particularly young students) are drawn to engaging with philosophical ideas; they yearn to mess around with big ideas. Unfortunately, we might also point out that young students come to the formal confines of school messing about with exactly these kinds of questions, until somehow it is conveyed to them that there are more practical (read: economically efficient) ways of going about being educated. Thus, the openness of such a question about what constitutes communication not only lends itself to a larger school context in which integrated learning foregrounds all curricular planning but also lends itself beautifully to musical processes of communication.

In this chapter, the concept of communication (as genuine dialogue) will lead toward a series of deceptively simple questions that frame a series of lesson plans that spark entry points into critical dialogue. With the goal of shaping dispositions that encourage interrogating what it means to be with oneself and with others, the step-by-step pedagogical strategies will be linked to the seemingly universal concept of lullaby. That said, however, the processes outlined and scaffolded in this chapter can certainly be transferred to multiple contexts and age/ability levels.

What Does It Mean to Communicate?

Before introducing any of the lessons presented in this chapter, I walk students through a kind of "mapping of our thinking" exercise. The purpose of this exercise is similar to that in the first chapter, where I modeled with the students how to engage with the other in genuine dialogue. This model extends this listening/response concept to a more practical and focused level, with the goal of practicing interrogative and probing questions that continually uncover other ways of knowing. It is also a powerful presentation of possible metacognitive strategies, as each person presents a question that reveals a way of thinking about the issue. Thus, students who may not yet have the skills to pose the kinds of questions that lead toward complex thinking strategies can learn from others. As important, rather than the closed (right or wrong) kinds of questions students experience daily, this kind of activity honors questions that perhaps may never have answers. If we desire students to move to higher levels of thinking that embrace metaphorical ways of seeing the world, this exercise is just one more strategy that moves them toward recognizing that for many of their classmates, the world presents itself in diverse ways.

For instance, here in Canada, where I have now lived for five years, the nation has recently begun to face its troubling and destructive history with the First Nations, Inuit, and Métis peoples, whose land was taken and occupied by colonial settlers. As part of this process, the Truth and Reconciliation Commission of Canada (2015) produced several studies and documents calling for curricular and structural changes to public education and the educational experience. Thus, a major goal in the decolonization of curriculum is a call to deconstruct biases, stereotypes, and racism inherent in both policies and practices. One can and should make the argument that the Truth and Reconciliation Commission's recommendation to deconstruct biases and stereotypes throughout curriculum and pedagogy is not only to attend to Indigenous ways of knowing but should also extend to all ways of knowing. Thus, "building student capacity for intercultural understanding, empathy, and mutual respect" (Truth and Reconciliation Commission of Canada, 2015, Mandate 63, iii) is a way forward for equity and diversity in all its manifestations.

Mapping Our Thinking

To begin the exercise, I write the following phrase on the board: "What does it mean to communicate?" I purposefully choose this wording, as it is vague enough to lend itself to multiple entry points. If I were to ask, for instance, "What is the purpose of communication?" there are immediate "right" answers that may dissuade students from grappling with meaning. On the other hand, "What does it mean to communicate?" both conveys purpose and invites divergence.

I ask students to think the question over for a bit (the often-neglected *think* part of "think, pair, share"). Students almost always come up with ways of addressing this question with responses I could never have imagined. So rather than give examples of my ideas about communication, I leave this completely open. Once students have been given time to write down at least two examples, I open up the floor to responses. I take the first response and write

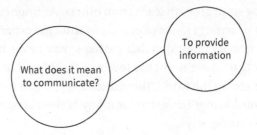

Figure 2.1 What does it mean to communicate? First step.

that out in its own circle. It's safe to guess that one of the first responses will be a version of "To provide information" (see figure 2.1).

This is where the teacher begins to problematize the responses by probing:

TEACHER: Why might we want to provide information?
STUDENT: So people can know what to do.

Timing is integral to an equitable class setting. Too often, we allow ourselves to be swayed by students begging for more time. Once students realize that time can be renegotiated, they will take advantage of this at every opportunity. You need to set a time and let them know this *is* the time frame within which they must produce something, whether that is a group or individual project.

Here is one of those questions that lends itself to greater introspection. I could respond, "Why do you think they don't know what to do?" which can lead toward issues such as language capabilities and so on (see figure 2.2).

But turning this question back onto the student may reveal thinking that is not necessarily linked toward a greater understanding of the other. Thus:

TEACHER: Why do you want them to know what to do?

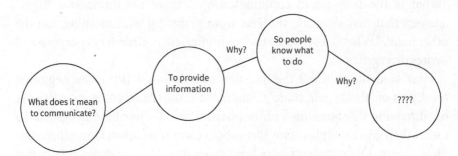

Figure 2.2 What does it mean to communicate? Possible next steps.

The goal is not to frustrate students into feeling they are indeed being "grilled" but rather to model this kind of questioning, which they've already experienced as we have practiced genuine dialogue with the other. Before the students become frustrated, I move to another response and open up the map to any place it may take us. Inevitably, I do want the discussion to move toward the purpose of communication. Thus, once I have modeled this kind of "why" questioning with the class, I have them work in pairs, mapping their responses while practicing these same kinds of questions. After a timed 10 minutes, we put the maps away and transition to the next musical activity of the lesson. The next time we meet, I open the discussion by returning to the board with the question that will move the class into thinking about the differing ways music is used to communicate: What does communication look like?

Communicating Difference: Who Gets to Sing a Lullaby?

In the unit below, I outline seven activities (with possible extensions) that provide entry points for young students to begin recognizing that beloved musical activities, such as lullabies, communicate much more than may meet the eye. Situating lullaby as a form of communication, rather than simply as something one does or learns, presents opportunities for genuine dialogue that might not occur otherwise.

Lullabies are favored by both teachers and young students. They bring comfort, provide spaces for connections to multiple peoples around the world, and fascinate young students with the often frightening imagery that seems so at odds with the melodic line. Thus, they provide the perfect texts for wonderment and dialogue. In order to help students express bias and misunderstandings, and even positionality, purposeful spaces need to be created and mindfully led by the teacher. Hence, rather than asking what a song is "about," pondering such issues and themes as family, love, bought and sold (or commoditized/rewarded) versus spontaneous love, and familial jealousy (and hyper-individualism) versus familial joy encourages teachers and students to wonder out loud in dialogue. *How do certain interpretations come to be shaped and normalized, and what that does that mean for those who hear and understand relationships differently? What counter-narratives might exist that challenge what may be construed as the "norm"? Indeed, is there an essential property of lullaby? When is a lullaby not a lullaby, and who gets to decide?*

Tight lesson planning should introduce a series of interconnected musical encounters over the period of time one has with students. The following, then, is a series of activities that can be inserted into several lessons over several days, as it would not make pedagogical sense to spend the entire 30 minutes of a music class with young students focused solely on one lullaby. Consequently, almost all of these activities should be framed by other musical activities in the lessons that set them up.

These activities are geared toward kindergarten through third grade (depending on the abilities and interests of your students). While the idea of lullaby seems "appropriate" for only very young ages, many of the books and activities are of interest to students in third grade and perhaps even older. It always depends on how one contextualizes and introduces these issues.

A note: I was able to teach these lessons to two separate classes of mixed groupings of second- and third-graders while their music teacher observed the lessons. As part of a research project, I was also able to record each of these lessons, with the goal of supporting the following plans. Without fail, after every class I taught, the music teacher would remark to me how impressed she was by the students' thinking and willingness to engage in dialogue with the other. If I could do this as a visiting teacher, imagine what could be done by the beloved and constant music teacher.

Unit Overview: "Hush, Little Baby"

Texts

Hush Little Baby by Sylvia Long (1997)
Hush, Little Baby: A Folk Song with Pictures by Marla Frazee (2007)
Hush, Little Alien by Daniel Kirk (1999)
Hush Little Baby by Brian Pinkney (2005)

Videos

"Hush Little Baby," solo piano, Joey Curtin: https://www.youtube.com/watch?v=8uCY3tsbkwk

"Hush Little Baby," Yo-Yo Ma and Bobby McFerrin: https://www.youtube.com/watch?v=GczSTQ2nv94

Activity 1 (Class 1): Whose Job Is It to Make Sure Everyone Has a Partner?

In this first activity, I lay the groundwork for the kinds of dialogue that build on the previous mapping exercise and think through the importance of small-group work and how to go about scaffolding working with others.

One of the ways to help students attend to the environment from the very beginning of class is simply to begin singing. I have found that music teachers spend an inordinate amount of time talking; more often than not, we feel we have to provide a lot of spoken directions. However, much can be accomplished through musical engagements; the less we talk, the more attentive students are.

1. Begin singing the song "Hush, Little Baby."[1] As I sing the song, I use a PowerPoint (PPT) presentation I made from a collection of photos/pictures depicting the words of each verse in the song from purpose-fully chosen photos that portray examples from multiple cultures and contexts that provoke wonderment. There is no text accompanying the photos. Sing each slide, and click to the next. You will use this PPT later to make a class recording.

2. After I sing the song once, I am interested in helping them think through the following baseline, beginning kinds of questions that will scaffold the way to more challenging questions:
   - What did you notice? (Rhyming words, repetition, one of the photos, etc.)
   - What is the papa doing for the baby, and why? (Help them focus on the word "buy.")

You will have to remind students that the goal is not to just exchange answers but to continually focus on the why of the response. Thus, before asking them to work in small groups, you need to model the kind of dialogue you are after based on the mapping exercise above. For instance, students might remember the cart and bull, to which you can respond by asking why they remember that particular image. If the answer is simply "It was cool," asking the students to articulate "cool" reminds them that the disposition is to wonder with the other, rather than simply agree. It is also to remind them that their thinking and voice matter to you and that you know and believe they are able to articulate more fully beyond simple responses. It is very easy to agree and move on to the next teacher-directed task. What is more challenging is to continually insist that the dialogue you are interested in is the kind that moves beyond the simple ticking off the box.

I believe students should work in small groups even as early as first grade. I feel equally as strongly that when we ask them to work together, they should be the ones who turn to those nearest to join without the teacher directing every group formation. However, we need to ask students to consider what working in small groups means (and the purpose) before asking them to do so. This is why I first engage in the mapping-our-thinking exercise with every grade I teach. Even after doing so, I often return to modeling how to go about thinking with the other before opening up this kind of thinking together. Beyond how challenging it is to engage in this kind of dialogue, we must first help them think through how to go about working in small groups and why they should learn to do so. Thus, no matter what the activity, no matter what the game song, no matter what the moment, I always ask the following question: "Whose job is it to make sure everyone has a partner?"

If I am to convey one thing in this book, this would be it. When I first ask this same question, even to a university class, the response is more often than not, "Your job," meaning it is the teacher's job to make sure everyone has a partner. However, if we desire a class community in which everyone takes care of the other, it cannot be the job of the teacher to do this. The problem is that some children, for multiple reasons, do not get picked as partners; some children are not immediately welcomed into conversations. And if it is the teacher who continually brings those students into the group, this does nothing to mitigate these offenses. Nor does it help to continually place the burden of care on the one student who can reliably be depended on to work with others. In fact, it only exacerbates the issue. Thus, we have to continually remind students to look around to see who needs a partner. This takes time, and this takes continual reinforcement. I know this, because it happens even at the university level (particularly at the university level), and it probably won't go the way you hope the first, and maybe not even the 15th, time. But if we insist that this is what we want, they will eventually take it on themselves.

> I once observed Gabriela Ocádiz present a workshop in which she reminded us that young children, who are still negotiating space awareness with their bodies during game songs, need to be reminded to look around and behind themselves when welcoming in others. There is nothing more glorious than watching clumped-together first-graders glance around and take control of partnering on their own. This takes time, but we begin from the very beginning.

3. Start singing the song once again to bring their attention back from their dialogue, and then open the discussion back to the full class, writing their responses on a chart. You will eventually want to compare these answers to future discussions using different texts. Further questions that can open the space for critical dialogue and that lead toward musical understandings are as follows:
   - What kind of song is this? Why do you think that?
   - Who might sing this kind of song? For what purpose?
   - Why might you sing this kind of song?

Again, the goal is to keep uncovering understandings with follow-up questions. If a question is worth asking, then it certainly is worth pursuing at length. This is particularly true for these questions, as they open up following activities that question who has the "right" to sing and may also lead to revelations of the kinds of musics that have been heard at home and in the community. As always, we can't assume that every student has had a lullaby sung to them, nor can we assume each has a home to go home to.

4. Sing the song once more as a class. (They pick up on the words very quickly, so I don't treat this as a phrase-by-phrase rote teaching moment.)
5. Find the time during this class (or another) to record the class (directly on the PPT) singing the song. If you have time or can work with the homeroom teacher, have them draw the images for each verse to replace the ones you have chosen. They love doing this, and it then becomes a class book they can have forever and share electronically with others.

Activity 2 (Class 2): *Hush Little Baby* by Sylvia Long

This book shifts the text from that of transactional love—or if I buy you this, you will do this for me—to that of a rabbit mom sharing the world of nature and the familiarity of the home with her baby bunny. The images are both intricate and often soothing, and young students love the message of the text.

You can either begin the class by humming the tune to "Hush, Little Baby" to get their attention or embed this activity within a larger lesson. Again, however, beginning by humming the song softly goes a long way as a transition either into or out of another musical engagement.

1. After students are focused on your humming, ask them what they remember about the version of this song from last class. Refer to the class

chart. Tell them you are going to sing a different version of the song in this class and that the chart will be helpful in keeping track of what the differences might be.

2. Sing the lullaby with the words from the book *Hush Little Baby* by Sylvia Long (rabbit mom and baby).

3. Open up the following questions to a small- or large-group discussion:
   - What do they notice that is similar or different, etc.? (There is no "buying" of love in this version.)
   - Compare the words and pictures in this text to the previous.
   - Note any themes that arise in the comparison chart.

One way to introduce thinking about these issues in more depth in this particular context is to model your own thinking-out-loud protocols in order to frame the dialogue:

Class, I have been thinking about the differences in the words of the two versions of this song we have sung so far, and I am wondering whether the purpose of the song changes if the words change. After you read some of the questions that helped me think about this, go ahead and choose two questions to think through with your partner. Remember that I am more interested in how you go about thinking with your partner rather than if you agree with each other.
- Who is singing the lullaby to whom and for what purpose?
- Has the story changed because of the words?
- Who else could sing this story, and what would change?
- What do you think Sylvia Long (the author) wanted us to think about/consider/ understand?

You can write these ideas on the chart or on a worksheet, start a thinking map, or simply just work though helping them listen and respond to what is brought up in class. Once you feel the lesson has worked its way through, sing the words from the book once more if time permits, or begin a musical transition into your next planned activity.

Activity 3 (Class 3): *Hush, Little Baby* by Marla Frazee and *Hush, Little Baby* by Brian Pinkney

This lesson highlights two distinct versions of the "Hush, Little Baby" story, both sung from a perspective other than a parental figure. The first may trigger dialogue about what it means to be "poor," certainly a topic worth thinking through with students of any age. The second features a family in which the mother is the one to go off for the day, leaving behind a crying baby and a father figuring out what to do.

Hush, Little Baby by Marla Frazee (2007). This first book is set in a decidedly nonurban context, and while its joyful images are filled with life and motion, students may interpret the story as one based in poverty. If this issue does not come up after singing the words of book, I would urge you to bring it up, as this is a wonderful opportunity to ask students to think about how the word *poor* gets both constructed and used. When I have had this conversation, even with young students, they are quite capable of nuancing the word *poor* and how it gets used and by whom. For instance, after singing the book's words, they have questioned whether someone is poor simply because they don't have fancy things.

After humming the song to focus their attention, tell them you are interested in how this story compares to previous versions. Note that the story begins in the illustrations before the text of the story starts. I sing this book through twice, so they have a better sense of connecting text and illustrations.

The questions I pose for this particular rendition are more complicated than those from the previous two versions. I am interested in helping the students conceptualize and name how voices can be covered, erased, and dismissed and, more important, why this may be so. As an issue of equity, who stands to gain and why this would be are questions always under the surface for interrogative thinkers. Thus, scaffolding dialogue that becomes part of the norm of a class begins early on, even with (particularly with) students for whom lullaby continues to hold great meaning.

As such, I ask them to consider the first question in pairs but then return to the full group for questions 2 and 3. So that they can engage with the text more deeply, I also go back through the book page by page to help them remember the characters and the story on each page. I have them return to small groups for the fourth question and then report back to the full group what they decided between them.

1. Who is singing the lullaby, and to whom? (This is interesting, as it is the sister, and the sister is less than happy when the story begins.)
2. Whose voices are heard throughout the story? (What does it mean to be heard?)
3. Whose voices are absent in the telling of the story? (Why might this be the case? What does it mean to be silenced?)
4. What did the author want us to think about/consider/understand?

Hush, Little Baby by **Brian Pinkney (2005).** I always include Brian Pinkney's book and place it along with the Marla Frazee version. This text is another glorious version filled with movement, featuring a Black family who live somewhere in a stylized, unspecified historical time. What's fabulous about this book is that the father stays at home with the children while the mother goes away somewhere for the day. The song is sung from the perspective of the guitar-playing big brother, hoping to soothe his baby sister. In terms of scaffolding, the same questions from earlier are used to frame dialogue helping students consider and uncover any hidden biases or assumptions.

1. Who is singing the lullaby, and to whom? (This is interesting, as it is the brother soothing the baby sister.)
2. Whose voices are heard throughout the story? (What does it mean to be heard?)
3. Whose voices are absent in the telling of the story? (Why might this be the case? What does it mean to be silenced?)
4. What did the author want us to think about/consider/understand?

You might at this point ask them to share their favorite book version of this song so far and say why. This would be a perfect question for practicing genuine dialogue. Rather than simply allowing them to list why the version is their favorite, ask them to practice helping their partner think more deeply about the reasons. I often have students practice saying out loud possible questions they might try with their partners before going into dialogue. For instance, "What about that story makes it your favorite?" "What about the pictures makes you like this the best?" Students always laugh when I tell them I am serious: "I want you to practice saying these statements out loud." I get them to do it, and they do always laugh, but they now also have something to ask when the time comes if they can't think of anything else. Eventually, they build on these questions without my guidance, which is always the goal!

STUDENT 1: The rabbit and bunny version is my favorite so far!
STUDENT 2: What about that story makes it your favorite?
STUDENT 1: The mom seems to really love the baby.
STUDENT 2: Help me remember what love looks like in that version.

You can have them move to another partner to share or bring this discussion back to the full group. Whatever you choose to do, I always tell students of all ages that we don't have to come back and report to the full group every time. The goal is for all of us to feel that we have had the chance to share our thinking with at least one other person.

Activity 4 (Class 4, or Coupled with Activity 3): "Hush Little Baby," Played by Joey Curtin

Until now, we have only looked at print texts. This presentation is a gorgeous solo piano rendition of "Hush Little Baby" played by Joey Curtin. The recording can be bought as a single, but the artist has also created a video to accompany the playing, which can be found at https://www.youtube.com/watch?v=8uCY3tsbkwk.

This rendition pairs beautifully with the Marla Frazee book version because of the photos that are included in the video. Many of the images portray children from all over the world, living their complex (often very challenging) day-to-day realities, including images from the Great Depression, Japanese internment camps, and children of multiple ethnicities living in poverty. This video lasts three and a half minutes, and when I present it to even the most boisterous of classes, students are mesmerized by both the music and the images. If you can't access this video, it would be very simple to create your own movie using Curtin's soundtrack, choosing and attributing images of children in differing contexts from all over the world.

After playing the video, leave a space of silence.

Recognize that the class will more than likely ask for the video to be played again. I would wait and play it on another day, because after viewing the video a second time, they may be less mesmerized and might talk or even laugh.

It is also important to stay away from asking the "What is this about?" question. If we ask what something is about, particularly when the textual imagery is metaphorical, we will get a report back about the storyline or a recap of what happened from beginning to end. Students are, after all, taught from a very early age to report back the order of events of something they have read. This kind of narrative ordering runs counter to experiencing the stories of others as something other than stated facts and events. On the other hand, I urge teachers to stay away from asking students what the story or song

> A note on leaving silence after we present music:
> We live in a world filled with constant sound. Our schools are particularly noisy places. Any chance we get to leave silence allows students to attend to and be in the moment. After singing even the simplest of songs, I work very hard at leaving a space of silence. Preservice teachers are always worried that if they don't talk all the time, they will lose "control" of the classroom. It is the opposite that actually happens. Humans of all ages are drawn to the power of silence and concentration. If we choose to be focused, intent, silent, our students will as well.

made them "feel," as there is nothing inherent in the words or sounds that can make us feel anything. We may respond in some way to what we have heard, and texts may allow us to make emotional connections to events in our lives, but words (and even musical notes) convey nothing in and of themselves.

That said, if students have never been asked to move beyond the narrative ordering, it can be challenging to help them make these kinds of personal connections to texts. It may take some time to help them move away from listing and ordering events, but once they figure out how to do it, and that this is the kind of response you want as their teacher, they love this kind of thinking.

Possible questions to present to the class for consideration:

- What did the creator of this video want us to think about/consider/ understand?
- How did the music support this vision/meaning?
- Is there anything you want to share that you thought about as you watched the video?
- How might an adult respond to this video? Why?

I like asking questions about how adults might respond to something, as it urges students to move beyond their own age. But do remember not to ac- cept a one-word answer as the final answer; continue to ask them why they are thinking what they are thinking. Again, this can be done alone, in small groupings with worksheets, or as a full class discussion.

I would end this segment of class by having them sing a gentle version of the song along with the class PowerPoint that was made in the first activity.

Activity 5 (Class 5): "Hush Little Baby," by Yo-Yo Ma and Bobby McFerrin

This would be a wonderful time to introduce the cello using Yo-Yo Ma and Bobby McFerrin and the title cut from their 1992 album *Hush*. Again, while you can buy this as a single, there is a YouTube version of a live performance that students of all ages love: https://www.youtube.com/ watch?v=GczSTQ2nv94.

I suggest accessing this video because of the unfettered joy to be found on the faces of these musicians as they play together. McFerrin seems to be able to hold his breath endlessly, which brings a heightened sense of musical intent to the foreground (listen to how long McFerrin holds his last set of pitches).

This is, needless to say, a completely different presentation of what we had come to think of as a lullaby.

- What has changed in this recording of the song? (Lyrics, tempo, form, etc.)
- Is this still a lullaby? Why or why not?
- What, then, makes a lullaby a lullaby?
- Describe how the performers are reacting to the music. Why might they be responding this way?

Follow this up by singing an upbeat version of the song. Use guitar or ukulele, and establish rhythmic patterns that the students compose.

As a future extension of this lesson, you might want to explore with the students how this kind of collaboration may have once been seen as odd, since cello players often play Western classical music. An entire unit based on the historical contributions Ma has made deconstructing what might have once been considered "appropriate" musical paths for classical musicians would open up the possibilities for differing kinds of collaborations. For instance, check out the wonderful footage of Ma accompanying the street dancer Charles Riley, or "Lil' Buck," performing Camille Saint-Saens's "The Swan" in Beijing on November 18, 2011, (https://www.youtube.com/watch?v=qfEYjKWJ56E).[2]

Activity 6 (Class 6): *Hush, Little Alien* by Daniel Kirk

This last rendition of our "Hush, Little Baby" theme, *Hush, Little Alien*, is by Daniel Kirk (1999) and is by far my favorite. This version of the story depicts a father alien singing to a young alien. It is particularly powerful because for a long time, it was rare to have a picture/storybook told from the perspective of a male parental viewpoint. The story (set to the tune of "Hush, Little Baby") depicts the trials and tribulations the young alien and father go through as they travel together on their spaceship tracking down a gooney bird for capture. Along the way, they meet two astronauts, visit the Milky Way, and have an unfortunate incident with a laser gun, all ending with the father tucking in the alien with a kiss good night.

You will need to sing the words of this book through once alone for the students, taking time to pause on each picture. There is a lot going on that you might want to silently point out as you sing. The second reading should be sung as a class, then opened up for discussion.

- What did you notice about this text?
- What is the gender of the alien child? How do we know that? (More often than not, the answer is a boy, but times are changing, and even young students are more mindful of thinking this through.)
- How big are the aliens? How do we know that?
- What does the author want us to think about/consider/understand?

Students of all ages love this book. I have read it at the university level to the delight of students who are happy to move beyond their jaundiced view of the world. This is a complex story, with much of it taking place in the illustrations, and thus it bears returning to over and over for even more nuanced points of entry.

Activity 7 (Class 7, or Paired with Activity 6)

As this lullaby unit comes to an end, I wonder out loud about all the videos and books we have watched and read over the past several weeks. I return to our chart and ask the students to list what they remember from our discussions (this will necessitate many prompts). I even ask them to write down their favorite three moments, so I can compile these and post them on our wall.

I then call their attention to the following questions:

- What makes a lullaby a lullaby?
- When does a lullaby stop being a lullaby?
- Who gets to sing a lullaby?

They talk these over with each other, again practicing our dialogue strategies. I time this so that they know each person has one full minute to share with the other. I then bring the "Hush, Little Baby" unit to an end by showing a video I have made by compiling multiple video clips that are available on YouTube depicting scenarios of someone singing a lullaby. Some of the things I look for in the video clips I choose are the following:

- Multiple languages, representation of ethnicities, and sounds. (Note that children may laugh when they hear unfamiliar sounds. I always take this opportunity to not get frustrated but to wonder out loud why we might react with laughter and what that might mean.)

- Differing gender identities, including males, singing to babies, calling attention to gender stereotypes.
- Siblings singing to siblings.
- Children singing to themselves.
- Adult children singing to older parents. (This always makes the teacher in the room cry.)

I always end this video with a dog singing to a baby. More often than not, this is a husky and you would be surprised how many videos are out there of huskies singing to babies; you could create an entire video reel using only these. Students love this, as it really challenges the idea of who gets to sing a lullaby, not to mention who can show care.

After showing the video once, here are some possible small-group/class discussion prompts. At some point in the discussion, you may have to remind them of the order of what they saw and go through each so they can recall details:

- I noticed some of you laughing during the video. I wonder if we can think that through.
- What surprised you?
- Whose voices were included that aren't usually included?
- Why were these lullabies being sung?
- Who was singing to whom?
- How might an adult respond to this video? Why?

I always show this video twice to bring their attention to details they might not have noticed before the discussion. A lovely way to bring this back to their own worlds would be to connect this to the creation of their own videos, whether that means finding their own videos online (with adult supervision) or recording others in their community (see the extension activities below).

Extension Activities

Certainly, introduce and teach other lullabies over the course of these other lessons, and make the same kinds of connections that have been made throughout this chapter.

1. Record someone they know singing a lullaby, accompanied by an interview with that person. Before doing this kind of interview activity (even with university students), I have the class brainstorm the kinds of questions that model the dialogue we have been practicing in class. We return to the problems with short-answer questions or questions that can be answered with yes or no. I often bring in the school secretary to model the kinds of questions we have brainstormed or might ask. Everyone loves this!

2. Conduct interviews with people about their memories of lullabies. Why might people remember lullabies after so many years?

3. Record lullabies that are sung in the community, and present these with their collected stories.

4. Write different lyrics to "Hush, Little Baby," draw the pictures, and make this the class PowerPoint.

5. Write original lyrics to a lullaby, and compose the music. Note that this will be made easier if you have introduced several lullabies and noted the use of language and imagery on a chart.

6. Compare lullabies from all over the world. Ask students to compare the themes that emerge in the lyrics of lullabies—often frightening images. Why might this be the case? What does this say about the relationship between caregiver and child?

7. Sesame Street has a fabulous video of Andrea Bocelli singing to Elmo. Waiting for Bocelli to take the octave is breathtaking and hilarious (https://www.youtube.com/watch?v=5BDVvB7Xx1w).

8. For a great laugh, watch "Sesame Street: Celebrity Lullabies with Ricky Gervais." This would fit perfectly into a discussion of what makes a lullaby *not* a lullaby (https://www.youtube.com/watch?v=Jc20vMz0V7Q).

9. Jewel sings a beautiful arrangement of the (Brahms Lullaby) with really interesting key changes.

10. "Twinkle, Twinkle, Little Star" interpreted as a lullaby lends itself to multiple conversations and musical engagements
    a. This is sung in multiple languages all over the world, and there are many YouTube videos of children doing so.
    b. There are hand-signed versions of "Twinkle, Twinkle" that lend themselves to the very powerful question: What "good" is a lullaby if it can't be heard?
    c. For Mozart's 12 Variations on "Ah, vous dirai-je, Maman," K. 265/300e, there are numerous YouTube videos depicting the score as the music goes by, so that students can watch the notation while hearing

and considering the variations. This would also lend itself to a unit on writing variations on a theme—including writing their own arrangement of "Twinkle, Twinkle."

d. The Piano Guys' four-hand piano arrangement of "Twinkle, Twinkle" is beautiful, with interesting musical citations within it. Asking students to mirror their movement with another might be a wonderful way to engage their listening to his fairly short video.

e. Absolutely, share Kermit the Frog and Don Music from Sesame Street composing "Twinkle, Twinkle." Students of all ages love this (https://www.youtube.com/watch?v=q1Ugqh471IE).

Final Thoughts on Dialogue and Meeting the Other

When I first began teaching in a way that created space for dialogue, I was concerned I would lose the musicking part of my curriculum. After all, many of us might see our classes once a week for 45 minutes, if we are lucky. What I have found, however, is that these kinds of conversations bring depth and meaning to my music curriculum and that students, once they come to understand how this kind of dialogue works, willingly move there without much directing.

However, learning how to do this is a life's goal and not something that happens immediately. I point this out because as teachers, we might be reluctant to return to something that doesn't seem to "work" the first time we try it. Of course, things rarely go the way one intends the first time, particularly when the goal is for dialogue between others. Being honest with students about one's intended goals, however, goes a long way. "Students, I just read a book (went to a conference or a workshop, etc.), and I really want to try some ideas that I think will help us grapple with being better people." Why we are so reluctant to share our own thinking and growth with students often speaks to our worry over a perceived loss of expertise or that we will have to relinquish control in some way. I always beg teachers to email me once they do share these kinds of thought processes with students, because the world shifts when you do this. Students see us differently when they realize we see them differently and afford the space for dialogue and difference.

Finally, I want to make the case that music teachers, in many contexts, have continuity with students that other teachers do not. At the elementary level, we theoretically have several years of their lives in and through our own. There is so much potential in the time we have, potential to help students articulate the difference between being treated equally versus equity as difference being heard and embraced, potential to unpack bias, potential to provide the space for counter-narratives, potential for antiracist work, potential for glorious musicking with the other. And wrapped up in such moments of beauty and profundity, opportunities abound for exploring what it means to communicate, to communicate difference, and to do so in and through music.

3

Friendship and Bullying

Interrogating Forced Narratives

The discourse of friendship pervades childhood. Beginning in nursery school and day care, "making friends" is the sacrosanct goal of socialization. This unquestioned discourse is continued into the formal process of schooling in ways that rarely, if ever, go challenged. We both come to judge others based on friendships and quickly come to know something is lacking in ourselves if we do not have "friends." I contend that this conception and this goal of friendship are so pervasive that they are often seen as the cure-all to bullying: if we can socialize everyone to be friends with everyone, bullying can surely be erased. This fixation, however, contributes to the repetition of fixed patterns that we hope to neatly package and solve. Our curricula are filled with books on bullying and bullying-prevention programs that, more often than not, are based on developing, for instance, individual perseverance, self-confidence, and high self-esteem. We are supposed to feel pretty good about ourselves and our teaching when we have the opportunity to check something off the list, but we know better. Not only do we know better, but research suggests that bullying-prevention programs "generally have a minimal effect on bullying and victimization" (Jeong & Lee, 2013, p. 8).

It feels almost impossible to disrupt the current discourse filled with mocking, disrespect, and disregard of the other. We see this on the world stage, and we are horrified when it filters into our classrooms. It feels almost equally impossible, however, to challenge the primacy of hyper-individuality, individual perseverance, and high self-esteem, all of which can come at the cost of the building of community and pluralistic democracy.

More distressing are the ways in which the pursuit of individuality and bullying that begin at such an early age continue, reproduce, and are made manifest on this world stage in poverty and in war. These are topics from which many educators want to hide our students. Yet these are the very issues many of our students know to be their day-to-day lives. Poverty is a fact of life for too many of our students. Many (if not most) of those same students understand the unjust conditions of their lives and grapple with the

Music and Social Justice. Cathy Benedict, Oxford University Press (2021). © Oxford University Press.
DOI: 10.1093/oso/9780190062125.003.0004.

ethics (whether they see this as ethics or not) of the contexts in which they live. While the United States is fortunate not to be currently engaged with war on its homeland, many of the US states do welcome the war-torn displaced into their schools and communities. In Canada, where the government (at the time of this writing) asks teachers to receive and welcome Syrian refugees daily, evidence and acknowledgment of lives brutally disrupted are a fact of life. And while I recognize this is a simplification, oppression of all kinds is the most ruthless of bullies.

What role, then, does or can music play in all of this? More important, what role can our pedagogy play as a tool for both interrogation and action so as not to "reinforce patterns of domination or patterns of cultural reproduction" (hooks, 2000, p. 391)? These may seem foreboding questions, but they are exactly the questions we and our students live daily, whether we articulate them or not. Paulo Freire (2000) reminds us that "To exist, humanly, is to *name* the world, to change it" (p. 88; emphasis in original). In other words, we must give students the chance to speak of their worlds, to enter caring relationships with others, so that, in naming their world, we help the other take on the tools to disrupt injustice in the world. Simply listening to stories, however, isn't enough, not through the texts with which we engage or the stories of others. Yes, safe spaces are important for sharing stories, but these are ethical spaces as well, ones in which our "ethical ought" calls us to engage our students in their world and the worlds of others. Genuine dialogue is one way to structure these contexts, dialogue, as Freire (2000) reminds us, that is "loving, humble, and full of faith" and that leads all of us "into ever closer partnership in the naming of the world" (p. 91). Children want this dialogue; they are desperate to speak in ways that challenge our notions that they are blind to difference, blind to inequities, that they do not notice color or disability. They do notice, and they do want to ask questions, but as Priya Lalvani (2015) found in her research exploring fourth-grade students' understanding of the meaning of disability, they had "internalized dominant beliefs about the goodness of *not* noticing—they had hitherto silenced their questions" (para. 19).

The texts (books/movies) I highlight in this chapter specifically frame and open dialogue that welcomes the questions of students and their recognition of the demands placed upon them by external forces, such as the pressure to fit neatly into narratives of friendship and bullying. Both teachers and students need to find comfort in grappling with paths that neither represent definitive answers nor provide a blueprint of utopic transformation. "Great narrative," as Jerome Bruner (2002) writes, "is an invitation to problem finding, not a lesson in problem solving. It is deeply about plight, about the road rather than about the inn to which it leads" (p. 20). Taking on ways of being and dispositions toward caring for the relation in the moment rather than for a future that can't be predicted or determined underscores a commitment to the here and now.

Critical Literacy

Janet Emig calls educators to action when she writes that "we must actively sponsor those textual and classroom encounters that will allow our students to begin their own odysseys toward . . . theoretical maturity" (quoted in Wilson, 2014, p. 69). In the article in which this quote appears, Beth Wilson is thinking through how to introduce literary theory to her secondary students. While literary theory is a powerful tool to come to know texts and our world, our goal here is scaled down to grappling with critical literacy and critical thinking.

Critical literacy and critical thinking are supported by most (if not all) North American major educational policy documents. These same documents support thinking and writing across the curriculum, the inclusion of multimodal texts, and the arts as a way of knowing. Many of these documents also support the cultivation of an informed citizenry who are justice-oriented, suggesting that without a focus on all of the above, including both critical literacy and critical thinking, such a world cannot be achieved. As Wilson (2014) writes, "helping students gain critical literacy goes beyond preparing students for exit exams, college, and work, to developing thoughtful, reflective citizens" (p. 69), but what does it mean to be critically literate? And what is literacy?

One way to begin thinking about these issues is to consider how often the word *literacy* is used and whether we bother to consider how the user is using it. Is literacy simply reading and writing? Elliot Eisner (in Eisner & Bird, 1998) would emphatically respond no: "Literacy is far more than being able to read or to write. Such conceptions are educationally anemic and shortchange children" (p. 16). This then begs the question, reading and writing for what purpose? Do we want students to be literate in order to communicate basic needs? To communicate effectively? Sure, but what does it mean to communicate effectively? To get people to do what we want? And if this is the case, how much or how little do we really want people to "know" if our goal is for them to do what we want? It almost seems that these questions are spinning out of control, and yet once we begin asking these kinds of questions (exactly like the kinds outlined in chapter 2), we begin to realize some of the issues at stake. Thus, it might be helpful to return to Eric Gutstein's (2006) definition of functional literacy as one that "serves the productive purposes (i.e., maintaining the status quo) of the dominant interests in society" (p. 5). One might argue, as my colleague Jared O'Leary and I have done (Benedict & O'Leary, 2019), that the recent push in schools to teach rudimentary computer coding is one such functional literacy. One might also wonder what the purpose is of teaching only reading and writing of Western notation to students who statistically do not go on to need reading and writing notated music after leaving school. For whom, then, is this skill intended?

Surely, we recognize literacy as the ability to read tablature, the ability to learn by ear, the ability to move knowledgeably within a raga, to realize figured bass, to create new sounds in a program such as Ableton Live, to harmonize within one's religious musics, to harmonize *with* the other, including, for instance, second line drumming and dancing. One way to reframe literacy, then, is to consider the importance of the interplay between multiple literacies and to recognize that "different cultural groups have different ways of making meaning" (Lee, 2011, p. 259). Thus, another way to think through critical literacy is to think of it as the ability for students to "move beyond regurgitating facts and ideas and begin to use texts to understand their world in transformative ways" (Hall & Piazza, 2010, p. 91). It is also to realize that literacies are crafted in the relational as well—the home, the community, school, and work. Thus, prioritizing reading and writing Western notation over all other literacies is to both ignore "the impact [these] aspects have on literacy development" (Lee, 2011, p. 258) writ large and reinscribe the colonizing properties of Western Classical music.

While shifting our sole focus from functional literacy to critical and perhaps even transformative literacies may feel like letting go of what we think we know to be true, again, educational policy documents are calling for us to do just that. And while we do not need permission from policy documents, to engage differently, including the activities presented in this book, as part of one's music curriculum is fully supported by multiple curriculum documents, across broad and varied content areas.

For instance, in its Vision Statement, the US National Council of Teachers of English (NCTE) includes a statement on "Agency," which contains the following:

NCTE and its members will be leaders in nationally recognized instruction, research, and assessment practices that support diverse learners in their journeys to becoming critical thinkers, consumers, and creators who advocate for and actively contribute to a better world. (NCTE, 2020a)

The Common Core State Standards, a defining mathematics and language arts curriculum document in the United States (from which the US National Coalition for Core Arts Standards were grounded), emphasizes

> using evidence from texts to present careful analyses, well-defended claims, and clear information. Rather than asking students questions they can answer solely from their prior knowledge and experience, the standards call for students to answer questions that depend on their having read the texts with care. (Key Shifts in English Language Arts, point 2, paragraph 1)

The National Coalition for Core Arts Standards (NCCAS) (2014) are designed around four artistic processes, one of which, connecting, calls for students to "Demonstrate understanding of relationships between music and the other arts, other disciplines, varied contexts, and daily life" (MU:Cn11.1, p. 9). Integral to the NCCAS vision is the creation of enduring understandings and essential questions "that provide conceptual throughlines and articulate value and meaning within and across the arts discipline" (p. 6). Thus, the following essential question, for instance, certainly supports addressing a wide variety of texts for such purposes in the music classroom: "How do the other arts, other disciplines, contexts, and daily life inform creating, performing, and responding to music" (Connecting #11, p. 10)?

And finally, in Ontario, two such policy documents, Ontario Language Arts (2006) and Ontario Social Studies Curriculum (2018), both articulate the need for students to move "beyond conventional critical thinking by focusing on issues related to fairness, equity, and social justice" (p. 53). Ontario Arts Curriculum (2009), while not specifically addressing critical literacy, does state that "The arts can also encourage students to be responsible and critically literate members of society and citizens of the world" (p. 4). Of course, none of the above, or "encouragement," happens magically. There must be space in the curriculum and a pedagogical focus on what exactly is meant by critical literacy both in and outside of the domain of music, with the goal of realizing that socially just engagements are grounded in reading the world *with* the other. Critical literacy at its most basic is the problem-posing education of which Freire (2000) writes, where

> people develop their power to perceive critically the way they exist in the world with which and in which they find themselves; they come to see the world not as a static reality, but as a reality in process, in transformation. (p. 83)

Texts and Pedagogy That Hold the Power for Transformation

The texts included in this chapter can be positioned as vehicles for critical conversations that address topics near and dear to the minds and hearts of our students: friendship and bullying. I have had multiple conversations with teachers who have shared with me how difficult it is to help students grapple with the idea of friendship. One teacher shared with me that her very young students don't really have a concept of friendship until they come to school—which indicated to both her and me that friendship, as students come to see it, is very much crafted by the ways in which teachers use the word and introduce and reinforce the concept. Thus, troubling the idea of friendship through musical texts is one way to help students think critically and ask the kinds of questions that help both trouble and navigate their social worlds.

Chapter Outline

In this chapter, I outline a series of lesson plans that offer entry points into genuine dialogue involving the ethics of friendship and bullying. From the seemingly smallest of engagements to the obviousness of poverty and war, music and musicking make their presence known in the following texts. The first section begins with lessons addressing bullying that are more appropriate for the elementary level. I first introduce *Chrysanthemum* by Kevin Henkes (1991) and *The Tale of Tubby the Tuba* by Paul Tripp and George Kleinsinger (1948). I choose these texts for two reasons. First, they both present clear examples of teacher/authority intervention and happily-ever-after endings. The second reason is a bit more nuanced and troubling. I want to remind all of us that simply because we read these books to students, our ethical responsibility does not end. Even when we have discussions with our students and they agree with us that we should be inclusive and get along and not bully, exclusivity and bullying continue. I know this because not only have I had playground duty, but I also have asked every group of students with whom I have ever worked, "Now that we have read this book and have had these conversations, will bullying stop?" The answer is a resounding no. Of course, it's not this simple; it's much more complicated. Indeed, a close reading of *Chrysanthemum* indicates that in the end, Chrysanthemum in many ways takes on the role of the oppressor as she laughs at Victoria (her main nemesis) for making a mistake during the final class performance. As well, a close reading of or listening to *Tubby the Tuba* presents students with the opportunity to challenge the possibility of quick and seamless acceptance from those who had bullied and mocked Tubby. But these kinds of critical engagements are within our students' grasp. They are their lived texts.

The *Chrysanthemum* lesson plans are meant to set up the issues that arise in *Tubby the Tuba*. I make note in the *Chrysanthemum* lesson plans (and many of the other lesson plans) that perhaps these can take place within the general classroom during language arts time. Granted, in terms of scheduling, this may be impossible, but it's worth considering for many reasons. The classroom teacher may learn from your pedagogy (and you from theirs), and the students will see a positive inter-curricular relationship. These kinds of cross-disciplinary engagements are also supported by learning specialists, principals, and policy documents, including NCTE, who recognize that when we ask students to think and respond in multimodal ways, all of us just might need to reach out generously to other disciplinary specialists.

I next introduce a book that lends itself to upper-elementary engagements. *Ben's Trumpet*, by Rachel Isadora (1979), is a poignant story (interwoven with jazz excerpts) of one boy's desire to learn to play the trumpet. He is mocked and bullied by others, and again acceptance is based on the intervention of an adult. I am certainly not going to suggest that as adults we should not be intervening on behalf of our students, but at some point (from the very beginning), genuine dialogue with our students has to reinforce self-intervention strategies *and* provide the space for honest interrogation and critical reflection of texts, both written and musical.

The second section moves from local bullying to the world stage and presents three very powerful books that address the complexities of war. At its heart, *Petar's Song*, by Pratima Mitchell, illustrated by Caroline Binch (2003), is the story of humanity made whole through the power of music. Indeed, one might even conclude with one's students that humanity is not humanity without arts and artistic processes.[1] *The Harmonica*, by Tony Johnston, illustrated by Ron Mazellan (2004), further extends the issue of humanity and what it means to be humane by asking students to grapple with how evil personified may also appreciate and enjoy music as much as those who have been persecuted and imprisoned. And finally, *Revolución*, by Sara (2008), a book that makes no mention of music and includes no words, brings these texts full circle into mindful improvisatory and compositional possibilities. What does it mean to represent war, insurrection, resistance, and death in sounds that further the images on the page?

I conclude with a third section presenting a series of lesson plans based on the 2006 animated movie version of Sergei Prokofiev's *Peter and the Wolf*, directed by Suzie Templeton. I have taught these in fourth grade through university, as well as in multiple workshops and conference presentations. *Peter and the Wolf* is a staple in many music classrooms throughout the world. My colleagues in Greece, Sweden, Brazil, and Norway (not to mention Russian and Slavic settings) all use versions narrated by actors from their home regions. In my own North American context, music teachers often use *Peter and the Wolf* to teach the "instruments of the orchestra," which, of course, really indicates the instruments of the Western classical orchestra.

> Note that the turn of phrase "instruments of the Western classical orchestra," while deceptively simple, is a powerful way to call attention to the ways in which we inadvertently reproduce dominant discourses, in that the "instruments of the orchestra" could very well mean, for instance, instruments of an Indonesia gamelan ensemble.

In Templeton's vision and interpretation of Prokofiev's folk tale, the beauty and power of the story forgoes text. Rather than using a narrator, Templeton brings to our attention the ways in which music can bring a compelling story to life, through stark images that call to mind postwar poverty in which the ethics of friendship and care are immediately available to all ages.

It is imperative that we see the texts we use in our music classes (and *texts* in this context means anything that conveys and constructs meaning) as a response to Janet Emig's call to action: "We must not merely permit, we must actively sponsor those textual and classroom encounters that will allow our students to begin their own odysseys toward . . . theoretical maturity" (quoted in Wilson, 2014, p. 69). I am reminded of a recent workshop presentation in Nova Scotia where a confirmed Kodály teacher approached me after we had worked our way through *Peter and the Wolf*. I immediately sensed anguish in her, which was confirmed when she shared how much she wanted to have conversations like the ones we had just had with her own students but was struggling with the pressure of teaching the Kodály sequence. She was asking me permission to let something go so that she might engage in this way. I knew this particular struggle; I had suffered the same throughout my career as an elementary music teacher. It wasn't just the sequencing, the teaching of music; it was a larger existential concern at the heart of her longing, the larger call of purpose, of why we do what we do with those with whom we have been entrusted.

Nowhere in this book am I asking anyone to stop teaching music. I am asking us, giving us permission, however, to purposefully craft and embrace spaces that disrupt given and trusted narratives, that teach ways of being with the other, and that honor multiple ways of knowing through the musicking we do with one another. Not only do we not need the go-ahead to do differently, but the socially just educator is one who uncovers permission as a deeply problematic manifestation of larger social constructs and sees them for what they are, what has been done, and what needs to be done as we choose to move forward.

Friendship and Bullying

Chrysanthemum by Kevin Henkes

The following two lesson plans centered around *Chrysanthemum* do not actually include any music making. If this is an issue, then work with the classroom teacher to present these lessons. Ideally, the classroom teacher would invite you into language arts class and allow you to run the lesson. How fabulous would that be? If you do have this opportunity, do take the time to fill the teacher in on how you are working on structuring dialogue so that they have a sense of what you are trying to accomplish.

These two lesson plans are meant to fill two 30- or 40-minute lessons. I implemented both over two class periods in a mixed second- and third-grade music class. That said, previous to this lesson, the students had multiple opportunities to engage in moments of genuine dialogue as outlined in the earlier chapters. While I see *Chrysanthemum* quite possibly following the "Hush, Little Baby" unit, it certainly can stand alone.

Brief summary of the book:

> Chrysanthemum grows up loving her name and the constant affection her parents shower upon her. After arriving joyously at her first day of school, she discovers how different her name is from her classmates' as they laugh and make fun of her. One student in particular, Victoria, leads the other students in this form of bullying, until the new music teacher is introduced to the class. After the beloved (and very pregnant) music teacher announces that she will be naming her new baby after a flower, in fact, Chrysanthemum, the rest of the students come to embrace Chrysanthemum as the musical production is rehearsed and presented.

> Note that I am giving suggestions for questions and responses throughout this section. You will uncover and encounter differing ones in your own contexts. The goal is to open the space to as many responses that seem reasonable with the goal of helping them think more deeply.

Class 1

To bring students into the class, I often sing an opening welcome song.

TEACHER: Class, I wonder why we always sing an opening song. Think for a moment, then share with the person next to you. Remember to ask your partner their thoughts before sharing yours. (Of course, I understand that someone has to go first, but the point is to continually remind them to think of the other before speaking themselves.) And class, remind me again, whose job is it to make sure everyone has someone to talk to? (Recall from chapter 1 that the task of creating class community cannot rest solely on the teacher, but rather all must commit to its importance.)

In previous classes, we talked about the purpose of lullabies and who gets to sing them. What do you remember from our classes together? (If you have not had this conversation, you can simply begin the class with a version of the next statement.)

I want to continue to talk about caring but in the context of friendship. I'm interested in your thinking about what makes a friend a friend—and what it means to be a friend. I'm also interested in the opposite of friendship. What might that be?

STUDENTS: Mean people. Bullies. (The teacher should absolutely ask students to think through what they mean by these remarks and to help them nuance these comments; however, I have not modeled that here.)

TEACHER: In the following classes, we are going to read a book and listen to stories that address friendship and bullying. Before we begin, however, I want you to do something special for me. I want you to think about your name, about your own name. Do any of you know why you were named your name? Does anyone have a story about how your name was chosen? (I always give an example so that they have a sense of what I mean. And I always give my own example, which is that I have no idea why my parents chose my name but that I know someone who was named after a movie star.)

STUDENTS: (Responses.)

TEACHER: Your name is very special and can't be taken away from you. But I am also wondering if any of you have ever been named or called a name that you don't like. Think about that for a moment. (Leave 30 seconds of silence, and time this.) I know that I have been called names before. I also know that I have been told just to ignore those names, but sometimes that's really hard to do. I wonder if it is the same for anyone here.

How you negotiate and navigate this conversation depends on the age grouping of the class. The goal is to listen and then respond with another question that elicits another reflection from the speaker. For example:

STUDENT: Stupid. I hate it when I'm called stupid.

TEACHER: I know why I would hate that, but I wonder if you will share your reason. (This response works well with almost any answer you are given. I am also aware that for some students, even a verbally expressed one-word answer is plenty and powerful. So I would not always follow up with a request for them to speak more.)

Today we are going to read a book about a young mouse who has a very special name: Chrysanthemum. In this book, there are lots of different characters I want you to pay attention to, but keep your eye out for the one who is a lot like your music teacher, Ms. Meren.

As I read the book, I want you to think about the following questions (on the board):

- Who are the real friends of Chrysanthemum, and why do you think they are "real"?
- Who is the bully in this story? (Is there more than one?)
- Do the bullies change, and why do they change?

Read *Chrysanthemum* (about 8 minutes to read).

This will probably fill the entire 30- to 40-minute class, particularly if your students have learned how to dialogue with each other, meaning that they are helping one another think more deeply about their responses.

Class 2

Have these questions on the board, and remind the students that you asked them to consider them in the last class as you read the book, and have them do so today.

- Who are the real friends of Chrysanthemum, and why do you think they are "real"?
- Who is the bully in this story? (Is there more than one?)
- Do the bullies change, and why do they change?

Students will not remember the book from the previous class. I always record someone beloved in the school reading the book; then this second time around I show the book as the students listen to the recording. Or you can take video of the person reading the book. This will take about 10 minutes of your lesson, but if you skip going back over the book, they will not remember the nuances in the story.

As an aside, admittedly, this kind of dialogue takes practice, which is why you continually go back to it and keep underscoring that this is the kind of dialogue you expect in your classroom. It may not go the way you want it to go, perhaps for a long time, but this does not mean you give up. You simply bring the discussion back to the class, and you work with them as a group. You could also choose two students, one who you know will do this thoughtfully, and let them demonstrate this kind of dialogue to the class.

TEACHER: I am going to ask you to share with your partner your response to the following question. (Remember, you want to help them think beyond their first response.) Let me demonstrate that with the help of Kareem. Kareem, what was your immediate reaction to the story?

KAREEM: I'm glad Chrysanthemum won.

TEACHER: What do you mean by winning?

KAREEM: All of the bullies like her now.

TEACHER: What is it about her that they like?

KAREEM: Her name.

TEACHER: Ohhhh. Is liking her name the same as liking her? Class, each of you has 20 seconds to think this through with your partner. After 20 seconds, the other person gets to take their turn asking the questions. I will time this and give you five seconds before it is time to switch.

Return to the questions on the board:

- Who are the real friends of Chrysanthemum?
- Who is the bully in this story? (Is there more than one?)
- Do the bullies change, and why do they change?

TEACHER: Now that you have had a chance to chat with your partner, I am wondering about these questions on the board. Who are the real friends of Chrysanthemum? (The following responses are actual responses collected during my research project with the mixed second- and third-grade music classes.)

STUDENT: Her mom and dad.

TEACHER: Oh, it seems a parent or caregiver can be a friend. Is that the same thing as someone your own age being a friend?

STUDENT: No.

TEACHER: Why not?

STUDENT: Because they're your parents and don't count.

TEACHER: (At this point, you need to make certain the dialogue does not become agree-or-disagree but rather new ways of thinking about the issue. Thus, you can continue to pursue responses such as why does a parent not count or move forward. You will always know best.) I wonder if there are other examples of who her friends were in the story.

STUDENT: Her teacher.

TEACHER: Everyone think of one example where the teacher showed care toward Chrysanthemum.

STUDENT: She named her baby after her.

TEACHER: She did, didn't she? How did Chrysanthemum's classmates react to that?

STUDENT: They liked her after that.

TEACHER: It seems that the only reason they liked Chrysanthemum was that the music teacher decided to name her baby after her. What do you think about that as a reason for liking her? (Dialogue continues . . .)

TEACHER: I am wondering who the bullies were in this story.

STUDENT: (If they remember the names, they will list the names of the classmates. I believe it is important to go back to the text and read again how the classroom teacher negotiated the moments when Victoria was being unkind to Chrysanthemum. There are several instances when Mrs. Chud, the classroom teacher, could have intervened differently. Which begs the question of why the author chose to make these decisions. Dialogue continues . . .)

TEACHER: Class, goodness, you have given me lots to think about when it comes to friendship and bullying. But I have one final thing I'm wondering. How does Chrysanthemum treat Victoria at the end of the story?

I return to the epilogue and read out loud. In essence, Victoria, after accepting Chrysanthemum because the music teacher does, makes a mistake during the final program, to which Chrysanthemum's response is laughter, which can be construed as bullying. This is a decidedly more challenging conversation to have, but it is *the* conversation to have with the students.

TEACHER: What do you notice about Chrysanthemum's response?

STUDENT: She is laughing at Victoria.

TEACHER: What do you think about this? Turn to your partner, and share your response. (Remember to ask them their thoughts before sharing yours.) I will give you each 30 seconds, and I will time this.

At this point, I often choose not to return to a full class discussion but to talk out loud with them about my own thinking on this. And I do not shy away from thinking through big concepts.

TEACHER: Class, I have thought a long time about this issue of friendship and bullying, and one thing I have noticed is that when the person who has been bullied becomes accepted by everyone, they often become a bully, much like Chrysanthemum is doing as she laughs at and mocks Victoria at the end of the book. It may have made Chrysanthemum feel better to laugh, but now it seems that she has also turned into a bully. I wonder why this is so.

Class dialogue follows.

Here is the leap into faith. It may seem that they will not be able to articulate this, but given the space and silence you will provide for thinking, someone in the class will come to the place where they say maybe Chrysanthemum doesn't know how else to act. If they don't find themselves yet able to articulate this, I would urge you to speak through a "personal story" where you once may have engaged this way. Speak to how those were the kinds of behaviors everyone else was engaging in and that it seemed "normal" to behave the same way. Note that this is exactly what Paulo Freire (1993) has articulated to be the case:

> But almost always, during the initial stage of the struggle, the oppressed, instead of striving for liberation, tend themselves to become oppressors, or "sub-oppressor." The very structure of their thought has been conditioned by the contradictions of the concrete existential situation by which they were shaped. (p. 27)

The goal is to help stop this cycle by naming it. And I would urge you to reword Freire's statement in a way your students will understand: "Students, sometimes when we have been bullied for such a long time, we become bullies as well. Why do you think this might be the case?"

End the class by reiterating how challenging it is to understand exactly what a friend is and to always be kind to others. Better, of course, than the teacher summarizing is for the students to summarize in such a way that all voices will have a space to be heard (e.g., written or recorded communication).

Tubby the Tuba by Paul Tripp and George Kleinsinger

Being able to articulate concepts, ideas, and themes that move beyond the superficiality of (for instance) friendship as "good" and bully as "bad" is one tool students need to cultivate in order to critically read and transform their world. Learning to question our own assumptions comes through a learned ability to ask different kinds of questions to all we perceive to be given or true. Thus, opening another way to come to know ourselves is through interactions with the other as fluid, always developing beings, or, as Freire (2000) suggests:

> Knowledge emerges only through invention and re-invention, through the restless, impatient, continuing, hopeful inquiry human beings pursue in the world, with the world, and with each other. (p. 72)

Asking students to engage with any text in such a way that opens up space to question (for instance) what the author wants us to be thinking, as well as the assumptions the author might be making and even what the author might be missing, encourages each of us to recognize the ways in which texts of all kinds act upon us.

Thus, while the musical context does frame the following lesson plans, the overarching purpose is to focus on the perspective of the oppressed other (in this case, both Tubby and the Frog), friendship, bullying, and authoritative intervention. Interestingly, in terms of thinking through fluid possibilities of transformation, unlike Chrysanthemum's behavior toward Victoria at the ending of the book, Tubby's generosity toward everyone, particularly the Frog, is worth contrasting and exploring with the students.

Tubby the Tuba is a text that could be used to introduce the instruments of the Western classical orchestra. Because the text and music do not specifically focus on thematic motives connected to characters as clearly as they do in *Peter and the Wolf*, music teachers perhaps incorporate this book less frequently. *Tubby the Tuba* follows *Chrysanthemum* quite nicely, as the issue of finding one's voice and triumphant welcome to the community, brokered by a figure of authority, resides within the overall message of the book.

Brief summary of the book:

Tubby the Tuba (a personified tuba) feels rejected because he never gets to play the melody. He meets the Frog, who commiserates with him and who also introduces Tubby to a beautiful and lyrical melody. Tubby brings this melody back to the new conductor of his orchestra, who is both surprised and impressed with this melody coming from a tuba. The rest of the orchestra, who previously had mocked and scorned him, now welcome him with joyous celebration.

Text (with Accompanying CD, 14 Minutes)
Tubby the Tuba by Paul Tripp and Stephen Gunzenhauser (2006).

There are also YouTube videos where the book is narrated, and the pages of the Tripp book are shown. Here is one example: https://www.youtube.com/watch?v=MTyNgHTFDfM.

Materials (Suggestions)
- Anticipation guide handout (see below).
- Flip chart.

Resources
A full description of *Tubby the Tuba* is on the Library of Congress website: http://www.loc.gov/static/programs/national-recording-preservation-board/documents/TubbyTheTuba.pdf.

Class 1: Pre-Activity Suggestions

There are multiple ways to introduce a text, including pre-text activities. Below are only two ideas I have used with class discussions. You may also want to include a pre-activity where you talk with the students about what instruments they may be hearing as they listen to the book. As you do so, you may want to ask students to predict what kind of personalities these instruments might have based on their sound. This conversation could quite possibly lead toward interrogating stereotypes that are often connected to specific instruments.

Two possible pre-activities linked to the friendship/bullying theme:

1. Anticipation guide. Based on the topic you are addressing, or the text you are using, compile a "list of compelling or controversial thematic or topic-based statements that relate to key ideas of the short story, novel, or play [or music] students are about to read" (ReadWriteThink, 2020). Of course, the statements you include need to be appropriate to your context, but example statements I have used when introducing *Tubby the Tuba* are as follows:
   - Teachers can always fix bullying.
   - People who have been bullied always become a bully themselves.
   - Once people accept you, they never bully you again.

   After students rate these statements on a scale from Strongly Disagree to Strongly Agree, they are then asked to provide a brief explanation for their rating. If you are working with students for whom writing may interfere with their thinking, then simply write everyone's responses down on a class chart. This decision has to be based on the level of anonymity the questions may provoke and, in terms of equity and universal design principles,[2] the decision has to be equitable to everyone in the class.

   After engaging with the text, the goal is to return to these responses to see in what ways their thinking may have changed.

2. Before introducing *Tubby the Tuba*, have the class respond to the following prompts:
   - What do we think we know about friendship?
   - What do we think we know about bullying?

In the past I have incorporated the thinking-map exercise (see chapter 2) with these questions to help students uncover depth and to think beyond their initial responses. If your class has done this kind of exercise, as they might have

Asking students what they "think" they know opens up a different thinking space. When we ask them to tell us "what they know," we expect students to conjecture in front of their classmates and announce with certainty what it is that they know. When we ask what they "think" they know, students realize the expectation has shifted away from the definitive to wonderment. They are no longer placed in a position to come up with a "right" answer or to rely on those they "know will know."

done with *Chrysanthemum,* you can always pair them up in a genuine dialogue activity.

Activity: Play the CD/Book or Recording of *Tubby the Tuba*

Return to one of the pre-activities as a place to enter discussion, and/or structure the class dialogue as you did with *Chrysanthemum.*[3]

TEACHER: What are your immediate reactions to this story based on our pre-activity?

STUDENT: I'm glad Tubby felt like part of the orchestra.

TEACHER: Tell me more about why you feel glad.

STUDENT: Well, the other instruments were making fun of him, and now they aren't.

TEACHER: Let's think through how that happened. Turn to your partner, and ask them to tell you how Tubby was welcomed back. And remember to think about his friend the Frog.

(Discussion . . .)

TEACHER: Class, what does this book have in common with *Chrysanthemum*?

Just as with *Chrysanthemum*, the tendency to want to sum up these books with a neat and tidy ending should be avoided. The goal here is to help them uncover the role of the authority in brokering friendship and preventing bullying and what that might mean if there always has to be an adult to make sure everyone feels welcomed. The goal throughout these lessons is to continually scaffold the kinds of dialogue and language that you, as the teacher, desire. Again, things rarely go the way one hopes they will when trying something new. When this happens, and it will over and over, we share with the students the need to continue returning to ways of being with others that places care at the center.

Ben's Trumpet by Rachel Isadora (1979)

Cultural aversion is the reluctance of teachers and administrators to discuss race and race-related issues like ethnicity, culture, prejudice,

> equality, and social justice. This color-blind philosophy is linked to educators' uncomfortableness in discussing race, their lack of knowledge of the cultural heritage of their students and the students' peers, and their fears and anxieties that open consideration of differences might incite racial discord or perhaps upset a fragile, often unpredictable, racial harmony. (Irvine, 1991, p. 26)

I begin this section with this quote in order to remind us of the importance of interrogating the privilege, assumptions and biases in our lives. What I am asking of us throughout this book is not an easy task, but neither should it be. It takes great courage to move beyond; it takes great courage to take action. While this quote may seem a long way away from our little Chrysanthemum and her insular world, it is exactly Chrysanthemum and her own inability at the end of the book to rise above being a bully (or the inability of the author) that reminds us that behaving as a bully impedes liberation, which comes only when all persons engage in actions that move toward a fuller humanity.

In North America, Black History Month (February) is part of the curricular calendar. The specific inclusion in the yearlong calendar of public education was the recognition and importance of the contributions of Black Americans to world culture.[4] When Black History Month was first introduced into public schooling, the concept of multiculturalism and multicultural curriculum was a much-needed counter-strategy to a Eurocentric curriculum. However, the point must be made that while public school curriculum has broadened to include multiple perspectives and points of view, the problematics of white privilege and colonization and celebrating one culture/race/ethnicity for only one month has to be part of the conversation you have with your class. A community that celebrates plurality, that *is* plural (which all our classrooms are), must include and represent multiple voices at all times. "Exposing" students (like being exposed to some childhood disease) to "other" cultures, as in "Boys and girls, it's the Chinese New Year; it must be time for the music of our Chinese friends," turns up way too often in our music curricula. As long ago as 2000, Christine Sleeter was reminding us to "stress the importance of multicultural education as a struggle against white racism, rather than multiculturalism as a way to appreciate diversity" (para. 1). This sheds an entirely new light on a month, week, or holiday dedicated to "multiculturalism." Clearly, these points should cause us a shift in perspective as we consider Black History Month or any school celebration that highlights one culture/race/ethnicity during a specific time. Keeping Black history to a period of one month legitimates white privilege and further marginalization. This serves to reproduce racial inequities throughout the curriculum and to "perpetuate a larger system of racism" (Huber & Solorzano, 2015, p. 302). Thinking through (with students) who benefits from Black History Month can help to "illuminate the ways in which black students may experience History negatively" (Doharty, 2019, p. 117). Units that are based on the development and growth of jazz are one such way to engage students in thinking deeper about slavery and the abolishment of legalized slavery in ways that do not endorse musicking as salvation, such as falsely celebrating work songs or the glorification of spirituals as rejoicing. And of course, we have to stop programming musics such as "Dixie" that originated in the "blackface" minstrel movement that flourished well into the 1900s throughout Canada and the United States. Indeed, including a unit on the minstrel movement would necessitate grappling with a time in history that is rarely addressed in-depth.[5,6]

On the surface, *Ben's Trumpet* (Isadora, 1979, a 1980 Caldecott Honor Book)[7] tells the story of a young boy who has a dream of playing jazz music (in particular on the trumpet) that is fulfilled by an unexpected source.[8] There is a quiet sense of anguish throughout the story that isn't felt in *Chrysanthemum* and *Tubby the Tuba*; and yet there is really only one page where Ben is teased and ridiculed. Nevertheless, that one page is enough to convey how powerfully hurtful and destructive one moment can be as well as provide unexpected moments and acts of kindness that can change one's life forever. *What does freedom mean if not the freedom to take action within public spaces?*

Text (with Accompanying CD, 5 Minutes)
Ben's Trumpet by Rachel Isadora (1979).

Materials (Suggestions)
- Flip chart.
- Musical examples of jazz from the 1920s.
- Jazz clubs in New York City during the 1920s.

Class 1 (Depending on Time and Depth): Pre-Activity Suggestions
Before reading the book, ask students to take note of and consider the following as they listen.

- The vocabulary ("cat's meow").
- The clothing (an indicator of the time).
- Where Ben lives (an urban center, most likely New York City).
- The sounds of Ben's neighborhood.[9]
- The race of the characters in the book.

This is the perfect vehicle to call attention to race and to not shy away from discussing the characters. We must, as Valenzuela (1999) reminds us, "deliberately [bring] issues of race, difference, and power into central focus" (p. 109). Thus, during the post-reading discussion, after dialoguing with students about the above questions, follow up with wondering where the "white" people might be in the story and how this question relates to the others you have been discussing. These are *the* moments when we can't be color-blind. We may have been brought up to believe that it is impolite to notice skin color or ethnicity or even religious practices of another, but this inability to see whiteness or privilege in society, as Mazzei (2004) points out, "produces silences that are meaning-full" (p. 30).

If the idea (assumption) of poverty or being poor comes up, and it will if you have discussed the above issues, this would be another great moment to help students think through what they mean by those terms—in particular, poverty as a social construction, meaning that poverty gets made by society and doesn't just happen. Students, even young ones, know there are mechanisms and ways of thinking and speaking that reproduce how people come to think of being poor and poverty. Unless we question with our students how "society" comes to define terms such as *at risk, poverty, disadvantaged*, and *culture*, the ramifications of these assumptions are numerous. And while it may seem impossible to have these conversations with students, these are the conversations students are desperate to have "with the texts of their lives" (Fecho et al., 2012, p. 477).

Once this dialogue has happened, listen to the book again, and help them think through the idea of friendship in this book. In particular:

- Who decides what a friend is?
- Who decides what friendship is? Is the trumpet player a "friend" to Ben?
- Do you have to have friends?
- What if you don't have friends?
- What is an act of kindness, and how easy or difficult is it to be kind when others are being unkind?

The powerful, systematic inquiry that is set up by reading all three books (*Chrysanthemum, Tubby the Tuba* and *Ben's Trumpet*) not only introduces critical engagement with texts but also affords organized and practiced moments for genuine dialogue. Here, then, is the challenge with the above kinds of questions. They can elicit short, yes-or-no kinds of responses, which are more reflective of monological dialogue, or Buber's (1947/2002) monologue disguised as dialogue. Our goal, however, in classrooms that not just welcome but also perceive the need for genuine dialogue, is both the space for these types of discussions and possible action points. Thus, depending on the kind of time you have—and again, this would be a perfect book to share as a joint project with a classroom teacher—extension activities should include outreach into the community. Whether this means a soundscape project (as described in chapter 4) or a short research project that has the students gathering, analyzing, and presenting data connected to one of the questions that seemed most pressing, the goal is "to create empowering opportunities for people to bring themselves to a better understanding of their world and their roles in that world" (Fecho et al., 2012, p. 481).

Extension Activities

1. After reading all three books (accompanied by the suggested critical engagements), the teacher should return to a conversation about the roles the different adults played in the lives of each of the protagonists in the three books.
2. After reading the book and having these kinds of conversations with students, the music teacher can certainly move to a more in-depth lesson(s) about the kinds of sounds and music they hear in the story.
3. Have the students create a playlist for Ben. What music might he be listening to? Students must also explain why they are choosing the music they have based on the context of the book. Students can share something they have learned about one or more of the artists on their playlist, perhaps even an anecdote that relates to Ben's story. This question and this book would fall perfectly in a unit one might be doing on jazz music.

Other Resources

For those interested in bringing children's books into the class, the following are particularly wonderful and present a wide-ranging view of musical and ethical issues. Of course, there are many more, and do share those with me. I have to say, however, if I had a favorite among these, it would be *Ellington Was Not a Street.*

- *The Bourbon Street Band Is Back* by Ed Shankman, illustrated by Dave O'Neill (2011).
- *Charlie Parker Played Be Bop* by Chris Raschka (1997).
- *Cool Daddy Rat* by Kristyn Crow, illustrated by Mike Lester (2008).
- *The Daddy Longlegs Blues* by Mike Ornstein, illustrated by Lisa Kopelke (2009).

- *Ellington Was Not a Street* by Ntozake Shange, illustrated by Kadir Nelson (2004).
- *Free at Last! Stories and Songs of Emancipation* by Doreen Rappaport, illustrated by Shane W. Evans (2006).
- *I, Too, Am America* by Langston Hughes, illustrated by Bryan Collier (2012).
- *Jazz Baby* by Lisa Wheeler, illustrated by R. Gregory Christie (2007).
- *The Jazz Fly* by Matthew Gollub, illustrated by Karen Hanke (2000).
- *John Coltrane's Giant Steps* by Chris Raschka (2002).
- *Nicky the Jazz Cat* by Carol Friedman (2005).
- *Old Black Fly* by Jim Aylesworth, illustrated by Stephen Gammell (1995).
- *Rap a Tap Tap: Here's Bojangles—Think of That!* by Diane Dillon and Leo Dillon (2002).
- *The Sound That Jazz Makes* by Carole Boston Weatherford (2000).
- *We March* by Shane W. Evans (2012).[10]

Bullying as Oppression: War

Three Texts to Encourage Meaningful Dialogue

> The moral implies that it is good to broaden rather than narrow students' outlook on the human scene, to deepen rather than render shallower their insight, and to enrich rather than impoverish their understanding. The moral means treating students, and oneself as teacher, as people worthy of educating and of being educated: who have minds, capabilities, and untapped potential that merit attention. (Hansen, 2005, p. 60)

Vivian Gussin Paley (1986) reminds us of the importance of being curious, of the "ethical ought" of being curious when it comes to the thinking of even our very young students. She speaks of her desire to listen and wait for the answers she could never predict, knowing students will expose "ideas I didn't imagine they held" (p. 125). This space of waiting didn't come easily to her; it was and is a process, as it must be for most of us who desire to shift our pedagogical encounters. And yet these shifts are welcomed by our students.

When we are curious about a child's words and our responses to those words, the child feels respected. The child *is* respected. "What are these ideas I have that are so interesting to the teacher? I must be somebody with good ideas." Children who know others are listening may begin to listen to themselves, and if the teacher acts as the tape recorder, they may one day become their own critics. (Paley, 1986, p. 127)

This is such a deep yearning in all of us—to be listened to, to be heard, to realize our thinking, our very being. Too much of music teaching feels already prescribed, already known, already written down. Yet, as Deborah Britzman (1991) writes, "When knowledge is reduced to rigid directives that demand little else from the knower than acquiescence, both the knower and knowledge are repressed" (p. 29). These texts and musical encounters I forward throughout this book make possible a move away from the already known and a space to enter more deeply the musicking we introduce to students.

As much as we would like to shield our students from the horribleness of the world, pretending that everyone lives happily ever after does not make it so, and indeed makes it worse. On some level, I recognize the desire to shield our students from the world, but it is their world, and my privileged worldview is not the only worldview. If we pretend that everything is OK, we remain willfully ignorant of the day-to-day lived realities of our students. I would suggest this kind of thinking comes dangerously close to seeing ourselves as rescuers. It is complicated, and it is difficult, and I know this. I know that as teachers, we want to offer our students a safe space; one in which they feel loved and protected, where they can thrive. But from this source of care, this "safety" may be preventing students from naming the truths of their lives. We may not be allowing the truths of the world and its history of both possibilities and destruction to appear and be named. Embedded in the life of this book, the words I choose, the engagements I seek to model, and experience with others is the following: in order to enact social justice, we must all be able to name and act upon injustice.

These last three books—*Petar's Song* (Mitchell & Binch, 1993), *The Harmonica* (Johnston & Mazellan, 2004), and *Revolución* (Sara, 2008)—address the ways in which "bullying" takes the form of war. Rather than write complete lesson plans for the following books, I rely on the teacher to engage with the kinds of dialogue that encourages curiosity and to embrace that meaning created in this dialogue will be "found in neither one nor the other of the partners, nor in both added together, but in their interchange" (Friedman, 1965, p. 6).

The first two books are appropriate for upper-elementary- to middle-school-age children. The final book, *Revolución*, could absolutely be brought into high school.

Petar's Song by Pratima Mitchell, Illustrated by Caroline Binch

One thing I find fascinating about this book is that the location of Petar and his family is unclear (although Children's Books Ireland[11] submits that "the features of the people suggest somewhere in the Balkan area"). While he appears to live in the country and the town to which they escape is not a large city, the clothing the family wears suggests contemporary rather than historical living. This suggests to me more current events of our world in which many families are forced to flee their homes and find shelter in communities they hope are welcoming. Again, the theme of care and friendship is woven throughout the story, but now bullying is made manifest in the hatred and bigotry of war, something much larger than what we met in the schoolyards of *Chrysanthemum*, *Tubby the Tuba*, and even of *Ben's Trumpet*. All of these issues can be thought through and named by our students, too many of whom have suffered similar traumas in their lives. For those who have not, we must help them come to know of the all-too-true realities lived by many young children throughout the world. *What does music bring to humanity? Is music humanity?*

Brief summary of the book:

Petar, a young violin player, always shares his music throughout his small village. His father, also musical, often sings songs with the family. Interrupted by war that approaches his village, Petar's parents decide that Petar, his mom, and his siblings will flee the village, leaving Petar's father behind with the other men. They eventually cross over a border, hungry, tired, but finally safe. Petar's sister tries to convince Petar to play for food, but he is unable to play, powerless to conceive of music in such a situation. Unable to find shelter, they spend the night sleeping in the cold. The next day, a man offers them a place to stay in a small shelter on his property. Although they are safe, Petar's deep unhappiness prevents him from playing his violin, as he worries for his father and the home he left behind. As he thinks of his father, he remembers his father's singing, and Peter begins to hum a new melody. He rushes to find his violin and plays the melody on his instrument. As Petar begins to believe he will once again see his father, he writes words to his new melody of peace, once again bringing joy to those around him.

The Harmonica by Tony Johnston, Illustrated by Ron Mazellan

This next book, set as a picture book for young students, belies the horror found within its story. Throughout the book, we never learn of the young boy's name; he is simply Jew. And while hardly the same, the importance of being named is an issue that was foreshadowed in *Chrysanthemum*.

We are not left with a happy ending in this book. Nor does the author try to sugarcoat the horrors of this story. We are left only the question with which the young boy grapples: How can a man so evil love the beautiful music of Schubert? And to add an even more complicated layer is to question whether the commandant is evil or rather trapped in a system that demands (for instance) his allegiance in return for his own life and the safety of his family. These are heady ethical issues with no right or wrong answers and yet ones our students can comprehend with the guidance of dialogue that doesn't seek to agree or disagree but rather seeks to explore.

Needless to say, there are multiple instances of these circumstances with which our students must reckon, particularly in the context of World War II. Beethoven, Wagner, and Bruckner were all revered by Hitler. Does this make these composers' music "bad"? Should we not listen to their music? If we do not believe in the politics of the artist, should we condemn their art? What does it mean to compromise, or not, for the sake of having one's music heard? These are the ethical issues we must help our students think through. There is no such thing as neutrality in anything we do, in anything we present. To act as if there were is at best to be willfully ignorant and at worst to reproduce inequities. To act as if there are easy and final answers to these questions is also to dismiss, at great peril, the incommensurability of belief systems. What we *can* do is to help our students hear the other, meet the other in their thinking, and to help them grapple with living with the infinite other.

Brief summary of the book:

The story is set in World War II Poland and was inspired by the true story of a Jewish family. This coal-mining family loves music and singing together. In their close-knit community, the family is able to hear the melodies of Schubert from their neighbor's record player. Instead of a piano that the young boy wanted so he could learn to play those melodies, the boy's father is able to bring home a harmonica upon which the boy learns to play Schubert. War comes, and the Nazi soldiers

invade their town. The young boy is separated from his family and sent to a con-
centration camp, where he plays his harmonica to keep from losing hope. The Nazi
commandant hears him playing Schubert and forces the young boy to play for him
every night. Having to grapple with how a man such as the commandant could also
love Schubert, the boy finally comes to understand that what is most important to
him is what his playing brings to the other prisoners.

Revolución by Sara

I chose *Revolución* to round out this series of books for both the depth of text and
possible meanings and the more sophisticated musical understandings that will
be necessary for the suggested engagement. While the story itself is not framed
or informed by a musical practice, its theme emerges out of the steady progression of the previous books. With a few words in Spanish, the story, like *The
Harmonica*, does not have a neat and tidy happy ending. Nor is it exactly clear
how the ending might be interpreted, leaving much space for critical dialogue
about what it means to engage in resistance and at what cost. Resistance to injustice, in support of (or as a form of) socially just engagements, can and ought to
be included in the elementary music curriculum. Preparing students to engage
ethically through and in action begins in dialogue and moves out into the world
as artistic possibilities for representation. And again, while there is no mention
of music, throughout the book the stark images and sparse text lend themselves
to musical representation and provide the possibility of reading and writing the
world (Freire) through mindful improvisation and/or composition. After the
summary, I present ideas for how to both scaffold and present this book.

Brief summary of the book:

> The book opens with a group of people gathered around our protagonist proudly
> holding a black flag with a red lion, clearly presenting a picture of resistance to an
> un-named oppression. Tanks appear and a battle ensues. The leader of the faction
> (the flag carrier) is arrested and placed in prison camp with surrounding barbed
> wire fences. An escape is planned. The lion from the flag comes alive and arrives
> at the prison to rescue the protagonist. As the protagonist rides the lion gun shots
> are fired. The book comes to a finish as a new white flag depicting the protagonist
> riding the lion is planted in the ground.

Scaffolding Ideas

Previous to any reading of *Revolución*, I make sure to have provided the
kinds of musical experiences students will use with this text in other

contexts. This means we have done (for instance) multiple improvisations and compositions, both free and with the use of building and layering ostinato patterns, created soundscapes, and improvised/composed sounds to accompany much simpler texts. This may mean beginning with texts where sound effects can be included, before eventually making one's way to books with no text (see the note under Extension Activities below regarding Eric Carle's *I See a Song*). Previous to this, I have also included Pauline Oliveros's deep listening activities from a very early age, so that listening and responding to the other has been part of how the students see themselves musically:[12]

1. Inhale deeply.
2. Exhale on the note of your choice.
3. Listen to the sounds around you, and match your next note to one of them.
4. On your next breath make a note no one else is making.
5. Repeat.

Call it listening out loud.

If you have read *Petar's Song* and *The Harmonica*, students will be more prepared to address the issues in *Revolución*. However, this isn't necessary. What *is* necessary is that they have had multiple opportunities to enter and dialogue about the issues being raised in the text before engaging musically with the text.

> I have done this activity with students as young as second grade, and the bottom line is that this does not go the way you hope it will go the first time with any age group. Young students, in particular, find this very uncomfortable and are not at all sure what to do with their bodies, with their voices, or with their attention. I often have them close their eyes as they do this, and after about the third or fourth attempt, their ability to sustain attention and create and respond to those around them is quite powerful.

You can do this by placing the first reading within another lesson, thus setting the stage for future musical encounters with the text. You might simply ask at this first reading what they noticed and leave it at that. Keep track of these ideas, as you can enter the next reading based on what they have brought up. If possible, leave a copy of the book (any book you use) in the homeroom of the students, thus providing the opportunity for them to engage with the text outside of class.

Open the next class by asking what they recall from their first impressions of the first reading. Bring up the points from the previous class, and list any of the new ideas. Choose one or two to anchor your next reading of the book.

Once you believe the students have grappled with the meaning they are finding together in the pages of this book, introduce the musical activity.

Place students in small groups. Have each page of the book copied so that each group can be assigned a page. Give the groups 9 minutes to come up with a 30-second sonic presentation of the page they have been assigned. I suggest 30 seconds because if you don't give a time frame, they will produce something much shorter, and 60 seconds is too long. Let them know that during the presentation, they will also have to focus on the group that comes before them, as they will have to take an element from their presentation and bring it into theirs as a transition. This has to happen in the moment, as there is no real rehearsal.

The components of this process, then, in summary:

1. Familiarize the students with the book and the meanings and understandings that have been created as a group.
2. Give 9 minutes to rehearse the 30-second sonic presentation of the page they have been assigned in their small group.
3. Previous to the class presentation, allow all groups to practice their pages at the same time. This is cacophonous, but it provides an opportunity for a rehearsal of sorts.
4. Place the groups in a circle so each group can see the other pages during the presentation.

Notes:

- Time the initial group preparation. I have noticed people seem to respond more attentively to odd numbers, hence 9 minutes.
- The first time you begin timing these kinds of moments, students will not be ready when the time is up. This is when you must not back down. Do not negotiate longer time. Go forward with the presentation. Students will rise to the occasion, or they will learn that you are serious and work more attentively next time. That said, this book should *not* be the first time you introduce a timed activity.
- There are students who always say they are done before the 9 minutes is up. Musically, you want them to keep revisiting what they have, so ask the following kinds of "what if" questions I learned from Janet Barret.
  - What if you added dynamics?
  - What if you added tempo changes?
  - What if you added movement?
  - And so on.

A discussion of "what if" should happen way before you introduce this book. This may even be on a poster on your wall. Get the students to continue adding to the list.

Make sure to follow up with a discussion of how they made the musical decisions they made, as well as the dialogue they had in order to generate meaning together.

Extension Activities

This same process can be done with multiple texts. In particular, Eric Carle's *I See a Song* (1996) works for students of all ages.

Michele Kaschub and Janice Smith use silent films in much the same way. In particular, they suggest *Say Cheese* by Derek Flood (https://www.youtube.com/watch?v=fkhsqzczx8c).[13]

Further Resources

For issues related to the Holocaust, see A Teachers Guide to the Holocaust, Music of the Holocaust, https://fcit.usf.edu/holocaust/arts/music.htm.

There is no dearth of examples of guerrilla warfare, conflicts, terrorism, and war throughout the world and in the Americas south of the United States. One might even tie this into discussions addressing the intake of immigrants in the US states bordering Mexico. For a look at the ways in which music has propelled resistance, consider reading about *nueva canción*, "a genre of pan–Latin American popular music, best known for propelling a powerful populist political movement—especially in Chile, Argentina, Uruguay, and Cuba—during the 1960s and '70s" (Gorlinski, 2019).

Multimodal Literacies: *Peter and the Wolf*

In their January 2020 call for manuscripts addressing multimodal literacies, the NCTE recognized the importance of the "incorporation of the arts, music, and drama into literacy education as well as expanding definitions of texts to include the written, digital, visual, and the embodied" (NCTE, 2020b), to which one might add aural and musical. This implies that *all* teachers (and principals) should value embodied musical experiences for their students, including listening and responding to texts that are sonic, visual, digital, and so on. There is no doubt that on a daily basis, our students engage and move fluidly between texts of all kinds. However, providing opportunities in school for our students to engage with multimodal texts is meaningless if we include them simply as a way to reach (entertain) them. Actually, including them just as a way to reach them isn't simply meaningless, it also serves to reproduce engagements that lack criticality. Students need to consider how texts act upon them, the ways in which texts position them. Thus, "more than simply asking what modes or multimodal texts *are*, we need to be asking what multimodal texts *do*" (Serafini, 2015, p. 413).

For those music teachers who might be concerned that bringing these texts into the class takes away valuable time from "teaching music," I forward a similar concern (substituting the word *music* for *writing*) from two language arts (composition) teachers: "Just how far can we sustain the push for multimodality without losing our identity as teachers of (just) [music]?" (Johnson-Eilola & Wysocki, 2015, p. 714). They go on to address two possible conclusions—two choices to be made—the first being to ask students to work with "words and only words," with the belief that these skills can carry over to what they refer to as nonalphabetic texts. The second is to choose to

acknowledge that writers, orators, painters, sculptors, videographers, and musicians all compose with deeply rhetorical practices, and, often, deeply critical and contextually aware practices—and that, just as written communication involves different kinds of visualization, production of nonalphabetical texts involves writing. (p. 715)

The corollary here is that asking students to work with "music and only music," with the hopes that they will transfer whatever understandings come from that into other textual domains, is certainly one way to envision the educative process. The other, they suggest, is to realize that by incorporating these texts as "potentials for learning" (Bezemer & Kress, 2008, p. 168), a deeper and more multifaceted understanding of music could occur. Thus, it is not that our music classes should become sites of honoring all other ways of knowing at the forfeiture of music, but rather that they should be sites in which genuine dialogue, sound, and image craft and create and convey meaning.

All texts are "carriers of meaning" (Bezemer & Kress, 2008, p. 166). Thus, if our educative purpose is to ensure that students envision and enact themselves as socially just citizens, then our pedagogical approach must "ensure students can actively and critically participate in wider social power structures that are reflected and created within text" (Rankine & Callow, 2017, p. 54). Suzie Templeton's 2006 imagining of *Peter and the Wolf* invites the viewer and listener beyond the Prokofiev score into a world in which power structures are fluid and hardly simple. Her stark images, both menacing and filled with care from the most unexpected sources at the most unexpected moments, draw students of all ages into a deeper reflection of a score and libretto written purposefully for children.

Peter and the Wolf by Sergei Prokofiev

Since it was first recorded in 1939, there is little doubt that Sergei Prokofiev's 1936 *Peter and the Wolf* (op. 67) has been a beloved source for music teachers. This musical story, intended to introduce instruments from the Western classical orchestra, centers around a series of decisions Peter makes involving capturing a wolf. Each character in the story is depicted musically by a specific theme, played by either a particular instrument or a cluster of instruments. Needless to say, *Peter and the Wolf* has been a fruitful source for the construction of lesson plans. Indeed, as early as 1945, in an article titled "Musical Development through Listening," *Music Educators Journal* suggested using *Peter and the Wolf* as a way for students to "appreciate real story-telling music" (p. 46). Fast-forward to 2019: Teachers Pay Teachers, a popular website that houses lesson plans for sale, has more than 299 possible *Peter and the Wolf* lesson-plan activities from which to choose.[14] If you choose one written by a music teacher, it almost always exclusively focuses on assessing listening or, more to the point, on being able to name and identify instruments and the musical themes Prokofiev composed.

Of course, this is what Prokofiev intended, as it was written purposefully for children: "I wasn't interested in the tale itself, but in getting children to listen to the music; the tale was just a pretext for the music" (quoted in Kelly, 2006, p. 7). I am not sure, however, that Prokofiev would support the hundreds of "fun" worksheets, cut-outs, memory games, and mazes (!) to be found on the internet. What place, then, does this unit have in this chapter, in this book?

Templeton's 2006 version, in stark contrast to the Disney version produced in 1946, presents a harsh, cold world, situated in a Russian forest on the outskirts of a small village or town. Instead of the usual spoken text that accompanies the music, Templeton makes powerful use of great spaces of silence and images to present the musical composition. The film, which won the Academy Award for Best Animated Short Film in 2008, is masterful in connecting small yet precise movements with Prokofiev's score. Beyond the musical representation, however, are the (ethical) issues that emerge in her conception of the story:

- Poverty
- Perseverance
- Courage
- Acceptance
- Cooperation
- Compassion

- Honesty
- Kindness
- Loyalty
- Death
- Societal pressures
- The human condition and nature
- Class divisions
- Friendship and sacrifice
- Bullying
- "Happy" endings

Clearly, each one of these issues finds its place in larger discussions of socially just engagements. Students are easily able to locate themselves in this story, as well as identify the ways in which Templeton's images mediate their understanding of both the power of the musical score and larger complexities. *What does it mean to be kind in a world seemingly bereft of kindness among humans? What exactly is a friend? What are the responsibilities of freedom?*

Teaching These Lessons

In the winter/spring term of 2019, I met with two music classes of seventh- and eighth-graders three times over a period of four weeks. Each class met for 40 minutes and had 20 to 25 students of varying abilities and needs. In the lesson plans themselves, I articulated exactly what it was I was able to accomplish in the time frame I had and also noted the ways in which the unit could be extended.

At this particular school, students had music only once a week, so taking a hypothetical set of lessons into a very "real-world" setting forced me to engage within set working parameters. *Peter and the Wolf* is accessible to students of all ages, although in this particular version, the wolf does, very unceremoniously, eat the duck (which I always let the students know will happen). I was a visiting teacher-researcher, so the students did not have an ongoing relationship with me; there was no reason for them to trust me or to do what I was asking of them. Yet, even though this was something quite foreign to them—listening and responding to what a person actually said—the students did demonstrate the kind of listening and responding I was asking of them. Even in the brief time we had together, they were willing to dialogue with one another and report back to the class on their thinking.

In one of the classes, there was a young boy, Alex, who did not bond well with the others, someone with whom others chose not to sit. He often made comments that seemed purposefully geared toward pushing buttons and boundaries. The other students mostly ignored him. I sat near him while we watched *Peter and the Wolf* and knew he was immersed in the movie. When I asked the class to break into partner groups to address the guiding questions, he was my partner. Alex reflected that the duck was now part of the wolf, and that was why the wolf had engaged differently with Peter at the end of the movie. I almost dismissed the comment (even though I have spent this entire book saying we should listen and respond more attentively), but in the nick of time, I managed to say, "Surely the wolf has digested the duck by now?" And he said, "No. That's not what I mean. The duck has become part of the wolf; he and the wolf are one now." Oh. My. Gosh. I was totally startled (in a way that I absolutely should not have been) to hear him think this through so mindfully. When he reported back to the class, at my urging, the students were as startled as well. Two things became clear to me in the silence that followed his comment. They were struck by how deep his comment was; they heard his thinking and the possibilities in his thinking. But I could also feel how they were struggling (almost unwillingly) to embrace this new way of seeing Alex. Minutes later, when others were reporting back to the class, the alpha student presented Alex's comment almost word for word—to which the class responded totally favorably. I wasn't sure if Alex realized what had just happened, so I turned to him when others weren't listening and said to him, "He totally just reframed the point you made." And he smiled and nodded his head.

Materials

- This lesson uses the 2006 animated DVD version directed by Suzie Templeton (approximately 33 minutes long), which can be found online.
- Flip chart.
- Index cards.

Had I had more time with the classes I introduced these lessons to, I would have broken them up and presented them over a much longer time frame, particularly class 1.

Class 1 (40 Minutes): Provide Background Information (Purpose and Story)

TEACHER: *Peter and the Wolf* was written in 1936 by the Russian composer Sergei Prokofiev. He wrote a story loosely based on a children's folk tale that he remembered from when he was a little boy, and then he composed music to depict the story. He wanted the characters in the story to stand out, so he composed a special melody for each of the characters, with one goal of introducing students to instruments from the Western classical orchestra. The work was premiered in Russia at the Moscow Conservatory and was first performed in North America in Boston with the Boston Symphony Orchestra in 1938.

Situate the story musically with a pre-listening activity:

1. Here are pictures of the characters in the story. If you were a composer, what kinds of things would you think about in order to write music that matched the characters?
2. In a small group, compose a brief snippet of a melody or sounds to convey each character, and present that to the class.

I compiled still images from the movie to help facilitate this thinking, as well as sound clips to situate the musical themes attached to each character. Wikipedia has notated excerpts of each theme (https://en.wikipedia.org/wiki/Peter_and_the_Wolf). That site also has clips of the themes, but they are MIDI clips, and the sound quality is horrible. A quick internet search will provide high-quality musical clips played by real musicians.

Situate the Templeton video:

TEACHER: In the *Peter and the Wolf* movie we are going to watch, the movie animator chose not to use the script Prokofiev wrote but rather to tell the story through the music and images.

Watch the first 6:35 minutes (stop the video right after the music begins), and address the following questions by providing examples from the video. You might want to choose from the questions and have them write something in response. You may place them in small groups and assign a question to each group or have the students work in pairs.

- What do you think Grandfather is thinking about, and what is he feeling?
- What different feelings may Peter be experiencing?
- What can we tell about Peter's life, and how can you tell?
- Describe the relationships between the characters so far.
- Describe what is happening (or what is being represented) when the gate finally opens up and Peter falls into the world beyond his home.
- What predictions do you have for the story? (Have them write this down on an index card or class chart for later reference.)

- What part of the video is going to stay with you until we meet again next time? Why are you choosing this part? (Write answers down on an index card or class chart for later reference.)

Have them first think on their own, then dialogue and respond to each other's thinking. Recall that the goal is for each student to further the thinking of their partner by asking "tell me more" kinds of questions that have been discussed throughout the previous lessons.

In one of the classes I taught, the students spoke of the possibility of death being foreshadowed, as well as the circle of life and the possibility of freedom once the gate opens and the music begins. This led to a powerful conversation about relationships and the responsibility that comes with freedom.

Class 2 (40 Minutes)
Have the movie cued up to where you ended last class.

1. Review the musical themes of each character. Have the photos up from the previous class for consideration. Ask students to consider what Prokofiev wanted us to think about/understand through his use of music.
2. Quickly review some of their predictions from last class.
3. Finish the movie, and return to their predictions (I typed these up and projected them without names attached to the predictions). Follow by asking:
   - What surprised you, and why?
   - What decisions did Peter make? Why do you think he made those decisions?
   - What effect did those decisions have on other characters in the movie?

You can have them write these answers down, and, better, have them talk with each other and share their thinking with the entire class.

Class 3 (40 Minutes)
Have the movie cued up to the last 8 minutes or so in order to refresh their memory of the ending.

The overall goal is to help the students tease apart the themes that emerge in the movie so that a space opens for an honest discussion about friendship and bullying.

Have students discuss in small groups and then return to the whole group. Choose prompts that are appropriate for your context.

Possible discussion prompts:

- The director
  - What did the movie director want us to think about/understand?
  - What is an alternative to the director's message? How would that change your feelings about the story?
  - Who are you in the movie? Why?
- Happy endings
  - What is a happy ending?
  - Did this story have a happy ending for everyone?
- Friendship
  - Did Peter have friends?
  - Who decides what a friend is?
  - Who decides what friendship is?
  - Who tells you that you need to have friends?
  - Do you have to have friends?
  - What if you don't have friends?
- Bullying[15]
  - Why do you think they acted as a bully? What makes something/someone a bully?
  - Do you think it's possible to make a bully understand other people's feelings? Do the hunters understand Peter? Do they understand the wolf? Why or why not?
  - In what ways does bullying prevention work or not work?
  - Do you think you've ever bullied someone? If so, what made you stop? What made you want to bully someone again?

Extension Activities

For Disney's *Peter and The Wolf* from 1946, situate the time frame of the movie. In post-video discussion, use comparing and contrasting:

- Compare and contrast these two texts, and analyze how their differing structures contribute to their meaning and style.
- What was your immediate reaction to the video?
- What were the differences you noticed?
- What does this version assume about the viewer?
- What is the message in this version?
- What would Suzie Templeton think of this version, and why?

- Write a letter to Suzie Templeton telling her about the critical difference between the two videos. Ask her at least three questions about the choices she made versus the choices in the Disney film.

There are several English narrated recordings of *Peter and the Wolf*, read by Eleanor Roosevelt, Leonard Bernstein, David Bowie, and Boris Karloff, among many others.

Peter and the Wolf has also been recorded in other languages. There are recordings in Arabic, Cantonese Chinese, Czech, Dutch, Finnish, French, German, Hebrew, Hungarian, Italian, Japanese, Korean, Norwegian, Putonghua Chinese, Russian, Slovakian, Spanish, and Swedish.

Here are some other versions:

1. Here is a *really* interesting version from China: 彼得和狼—Bǐdé hé láng, https://www.youtube.com/watch?v=kLk873XqY5o. In this animated version, you see a familiar story enacted, but the music is *not* the Prokofiev score. There are, however, citations from the original score, so in many ways, the essence of Prokofiev is there—but not. I would absolutely introduce this version in comparison.
2. In Russian: https://www.youtube.com/watch?v=r-1OWPWzCMM.
3. In Portuguese: *Pedro e o Lobo*, https://www.youtube.com/watch?v=ggRJRSJvFTA.
4. A jazz version: https://www.youtube.com/watch?v=zMNzL5tMwRM. This is a complete *Peter and the Wolf* score arranged for jazz ensemble by Walter Gwardyak, with modern libretto by Giacomo Gates.
5. A New Orleans–style jazz band from Glasgow, Scotland: https://www.youtube.com/watch?v=s9k1VRuil4Q.
6. Bono created a version for the Irish Hospice Foundation: http://www.peterwolf.org/home.html. There is also an interesting YouTube video of the creation process: https://www.youtube.com/watch?v=wTsTwIHfRME.

Further Class Composition Activity

Have students choose a story and compose musical themes for each character, using voices, found instruments, classroom instruments, or even technology. They should be prepared to explain their compositional choices to the class. Perform this in small groups or as a class. Connect these musical themes with the literary themes found in the story, which may be similar to or different from those discussed in *Peter and the Wolf*.

Lingering Issues

This chapter covers a lot of ground, from the almost innocent world of Chrysanthemum, moving through worlds of war and revolution, and ending firmly on the ethical grounding of Peter and his "friend" the wolf. As I look back and contemplate the issues raised, I am reminded of how powerful the words are that we choose to use, how powerfully children interpret them and construct their own understandings based on our words. I no longer use the word *friend* or *friends* when I engage with students. I think of my daughter. It was never easy for her to make friends the way I did, the way I expected her to. I recognize, perhaps too late, the damage done when she would come home from school and I would continually ask about friends. The expectation of friendship wears on all of us. This should not be a burden. Learning to be with the other, to come to understand the other, as Peter did with the wolf, actually feels less burdensome, within our reach, and far more powerful.

The differing kinds of literacies presented throughout this chapter offer spaces for wonderment rather than definitive knowing, dialogue that can lead to humility, spaces for pause that can help us interrogate biases, privilege, and power. These literacies (located in our pedagogy) encourage us to live more generously in a pluralistic world as socially just citizens. Found within the most seemingly small gestures, *particularly* in the most seemingly small gestures, socially just engagements begin as we look around and know without pause whose job it is to make sure everyone has a partner: it is our job.

4

Soundscapes

Listening for Meaningful Relationships—
In Conversation with Kelly Bylica

The first time I watched Kelly Bylica teach was on a study-abroad trip in Guatemala. The goal of the trip was to encourage a group of undergraduates both to interrogate ideas they may have had linked to salvation narratives of teaching and to help them grapple with genuine dialogue, as made possible through our engagements with teachers and students throughout Guatemala.

As we made our way through schools of all levels, most, if not all, situated in high levels of poverty, we found many opportunities to make music with everyone we met. In our conversations and the journals the students kept, we began to notice the frustration students felt at what they referred to as a "barrier" to communication. The undergraduates kept returning to how they were unable to *make* the Guatemalan students and musicians understand what *they* wanted them to understand. As you can imagine after reading the first chapters in this book, helping them to interrogate this idea of barrier, as well as the (colonizing) power dynamic they were assuming, became a major and recurring pedagogical intent.

Throughout this trip, Kelly modeled to the undergraduates ways of being with others and making and creating music without the need to use words. She did this simply as an extension of who she is, which made a powerful impression on those undergraduates. So for me, inviting her here to talk about her work with soundscapes as a vehicle for interrogation makes perfect sense. But first, we might wonder what exactly makes a soundscape a soundscape.

I am ashamed to admit that when I was living and teaching in the United States, I had only peripherally heard of the work of Canadian composer R. Murray Schafer. Living now in Canada, I have come to know more intimately his way of both hearing and seeing the world, particularly through the musical context of a soundscape. Many of us have undoubtedly used soundscapes in our music classrooms for multiple purposes. Certainly, they are a way to connect students to compositional processes. But in a book such as this, where the focus is on genuine dialogue with our students, it makes

Music and Social Justice. Cathy Benedict, Oxford University Press (2021). © Oxford University Press.
DOI: 10.1093/oso/9780190062125.003.0005.

sense to think of soundscapes as our guest author does, as a way to create possibilities for challenging the ways we think about music, about listening, and about understanding our world and those of others.

There are many ways to define a soundscape, but Kelly (using the work of musician-scholars) helps us think of them as the following:

"The total field of sounds wherever you are" (Schafer, 1992, p. 8).

"Waveforms faithfully transmitted to our cortex by the ear and its mechanisms" (Oliveros, 2005, p. 18).

"[The ways in which] the environment is understood by those living within it" (Truax, 2001, p. 11).

And while this helps us conceptualize our topic at hand theoretically, what is really powerful to note is that the sound composition itself is only part of the story. As researchers Hall et al. (2008) remind us, soundscapes are not only audible sounds. They are also the ways in which we use the amalgamation of those sounds to tell stories, make meaning, and help us reflect on what and how we hear that makes this chapter so valuable in a book such as this.

In the following pages, Kelly provides a flexible outline of a lived-experience soundscape project with guiding questions and examples of potential dialogue. In addition to the development of compositional and musical skills, she also offers ways of engaging students in listening. As has been (and will be) reinforced throughout the book, listening, as a complex and developed skill, is more than the taking in of presented information. Rather, listening is essential to the co-construction of a mutual relationship. How perfect, then, is the work of Kelly as she helps us explore the ways sound can help us think, learn, and be in relation with others.

Soundscapes and Social Responsibility— By Kelly Bylica

When I first began working with soundscapes in my general music and choral classes, they manifested as the recreation of particular environments. We used recordings or live imitative sounds for the purpose of exploring the sonic nature of a context such as a basketball game, rainstorm, or city street. These soundscapes might be used to complement repertoire or serve as a compositional entry point for students. I found these initial forays into soundscapes to be creative in that students often developed their own ideas and interpreted the activity and prompt in whatever way they chose. I did not assign a checklist to complete or a rubric to fill out. These early ventures encouraged an openness toward listening to the sounds of the world and challenged what students often understood as "traditional" (i.e., notation-based) composition. However, I felt something was missing. *We may have been listening differently, but what did that really mean, and to what end? What was the greater purpose beyond creative engagement?*

Schafer has often championed soundscapes as a space to discuss personal social responsibility and consider the possibilities of our relationship with the world. An environmental advocate, he believes that humans have an ethical imperative to care for the planet, particularly as the world becomes a more crowded, cacophonous place. For me, social responsibility is also about our relationship with the other in terms of how we listen to and care for one another. Drawing on these ideas, I became interested in how I might extend Schafer's thinking into my own pedagogical practices.

Here I present one possibility that I experimented with in my own classroom, using soundscape compositions to help students and educators consider what it means to listen to ourselves, others, and our world. What I offer is not meant to be a recipe or a push for a classroom curriculum that focuses solely on composition. It is also not an articulation of the nuances, particularities, and complexities of engaging with a project such as this in different contexts with unique human beings. Rather, my hope is that it prompts questions, ideas, and dialogue about our relationships with the world, each other, and ourselves.

Lived-Experience Soundscapes: The Project

As a precursor to the project, I like to start by first asking students to *think* about listening. Thus, rather than begin by listening to the world and the environment, I ask them to consider what it might mean to listen to one another. I emphasize the need to explore listening not only because I believe we *should* be talking about how we can listen to one another but also because students will be creating these lived-experience compositions with sounds from their own personal lives and experiences. Their stories may quite possibly be intimate, and it is part of our ethical responsibility as educators to create space for those stories to be heard and shared. Maxine Greene (1995) writes of

the importance of freeing our children to tell their stories, not only so we can hear them but so that they can make meaningful the birth of their own rationality. It may remind us, too, of the importance of affirming many kinds of experience, even those that seem incompatible with our own interpretations of the world. (p. 54)

Often students spend the majority of their day in situations of "forced listening" (Cumberland, 2001), where they are instructed on where to turn their attention and how to spend their time. They are told whose stories they should listen to and how those stories should be interpreted. This often results in some students choosing to follow the "shoulds" of listening and others choosing not to listen at all. In our conversations together, I ask them to consider that listening is above all an act of care.

While the project takes shape differently each time, I have a few prompts I often use to begin conversations about listening as a form of care: *What does it mean to listen? When do you feel listened to? What does it feel like to be listened to? Or not listened to? Do you know anyone who always cuts you off when you talk? Or someone who always has a better tale to tell or "one-ups" your own story? How does that make you feel? How can we show care through listening?*[1] Hands go up as students are quick to share a list of those people, often adults, who they feel do not listen to them.

Deliberately seeking to help students grapple with how they come to understand their own world, I ask them to journal about these prompts, as well as to think through their responses to such questions as:

- How do I hear home?
- How do I hear my community?
- How do I make meaning from my sonic environment?

And while journaling is a powerful way to frame one's thinking more often than not, I also choose to have them discuss in small groups, practicing listening and questioning skills. As Cathy describes in chapter 1, I, too, model what this might look like with the class as a whole, emphasizing that there are no "right" answers or interpretations, that the goal is to affirm and recognize many kinds of experiences and interpretations.

Step 1: Listening to the World

Listening to their world helps students situate themselves within the fluid landscapes of their own experiences, contexts, and, ultimately, soundscapes. At this stage, I often ask students to keep a listening journal of sounds they hear during the day in various contexts and situations or even sounds that occur to them in their minds as they recall memories or experiences. Sometimes we classify these, for instance, sounds I like, sounds that are joyous, thinking sounds, scary sounds, and so on. I often find myself doing these classifications when I enter a new space or when I am waiting for a train or walking through a city, and I encourage you to do the same as an educator. How often do we really pause to listen to the world around us? In fact, I often participate in this project alongside students, recognizing the need to consider "the notion of *who we are* as teachers" (Benedict, 2006, p. 3; emphasis in original) and how that helps shape our epistemologies and the ways in which we, too, see students and our world.

Students then start to develop sound lists for their compositions from their listening journals. *What sounds do they find meaningful? Why? How do these sounds help represent how they hear their world? How might they see themselves as composers who are intending not only to inform but also to provoke and stimulate?* Student lists are often peppered with a wide variety of sounds, from school bells to lullabies, barking dogs to religious hymns and prayer calls. Lists then turn into recordings, as students record or create audio clips to be used in their compositions. These recordings might take place outside of school on cell phones or recording devices that are then uploaded to school computers. Or they might be found on one of many free audio clip websites or recorded during the school day.

Step 2: From Sounds to Composition— Uploading and Mixing

We then take the recorded sounds and audio clips and begin the process of creatively turning them into meaningful compositions that tell stories, share interpretations, and, ideally, inspire dialogue and new ways of thinking. There are a variety of ways to enter this process. If your school has access to any one of a variety of technological options, you might consider using resources such as GarageBand, Soundtrap, Soundation, or WeVideo. Students can upload the sounds to school devices and explore tension and release, volume, pitch, layering, and other digital mixing skills in order to create their musical compositions.

If you do not have access to technology or prefer to have students create their soundscapes live, the recorded sounds can be recreated by using classroom instruments or items found around school.

Perhaps they will work in a group, with each student working as both composer for their own composition and performer for the compositions of others. *How does listening work differently in these environments? How does the role we play in each context impact how we listen?* Through the compositional process, be it technologically based or not, students are playing with possibilities for constructing, deconstructing, and reconstructing sounds and musical ideas.

Step 3: Remixing and Revising

While composing, students and teachers can practice helping one another reflect on the choices made through the listening and questioning processes discussed earlier. *Why did you choose to use this sound here? What might change? Were all of your choices purposeful? In what ways?* In small groups, students might listen to a snippet of a classmate's work in progress, helping one another reflect and engage in an ongoing process of revision. Furthermore, journal prompts can be offered that encourage students to introspectively ask questions of themselves, such as: *What questions do you hope your composition will elicit or inspire? Is this helping you think about your own perspective differently? How?*

During this process, I also challenge you, the educator, to let go of any preconceived notions of what the musical outcome will be in students' compositions. *How might you maintain an openness that allows for a multitude of ways of interpreting and responding to this prompt?*

Step 4: Sharing, Provoking, Reflecting

Once students have had the opportunity to explore, discuss, revise, and remix their compositions, the typical progression in a classroom project is usually to ask the students to present their pieces. If the goal of engaging in these compositions is to generate dialogue and reflection, a simple "Here's my composition" followed by a "What did you like? What would you change?" moment is not likely to be fulfilling. In fact, I would argue that this type of presentation often results in unengaged, uncritical performances, where the only skill learned is how to stand up in front of one's peers, regardless of the project. Not to belittle this skill, but perhaps we might consider an alternative. I am suggesting that we play (or perform) each student's composition two or three times (or as many times as needed through a listening walk), allowing listeners the opportunity to reflect individually and communally on what they heard through dialogue or journaling. What if instead of prompting them with "What did you like?" and "What would you change?" we asked: *What did you notice? What do you wonder? How might someone else interpret this differently? What are you thinking about as you listen? Are there larger issues that this brings up for you? What might you ask the composer?* This could then be followed with a group conversation addressing the different lenses through which the piece was viewed.

Extensions

Extensions and possibilities for this project abound. Students might pair photographs or visuals with their composition. They might add text or story-writing. Consider asking them to interview someone as part of the project, someone who is a regular part of their world, such as a family member, or someone they perceive as possibly living in a different space from themselves. Students could write the interview questions individually or collaboratively as a class, or they could create a list of questions from which to choose.

This project also lends itself to collaboration between communities. You might reach out to a community that differs from your own. If you teach in a rural environment, consider an urban school. If you teach students on the West Coast, consider a Midwestern or Southern school. If you teach in the suburbs, consider partnering with a school on a First Nations reserve. You might even consider partnering with a school in another country. Exploring different communities is not about labeling these communities as "other" but about thinking through how our contexts and experiences shape how we see the world. The questions might be larger in scope, but the overarching purpose is the same. *How are the ways in which we understand our world impacted by our own experiences, positionalities, and assumptions? How might we explore this musically?*

Concluding Thoughts

What is offered here is not a how-to or a formula but rather a look into my own processes and how I came to work with soundscape projects in this particular manner. I found in my experiences that students in the music classes I taught were eager to be listened to, keen to build relationships, interested in sharing their experiences, and willing to hear and debate multiple interpretations and viewpoints. They came from different backgrounds, cultures, races, ethnicities, and experiences, but rarely were these differences engaged with openly and purposefully. Difference deserves to be named and explored, "to engage with the complexities of a world populated by Others who are not like us" (Biesta, 2010, p. 85). Thus, I believe we are obligated to create ways to meaningfully engage with such differences through musical engagements. The goal of the artist—the student composer—is not only to creatively bring something new into the world but also to use this composition to draw attention to how varying individual interpretations and lived experiences can help us understand the webs of sociopolitical, cultural, and economic power relations that permeate our lives.

This is just one entry point or example of how we might engage meaningfully and purposefully with students in the music classroom. In particular, this project promotes an environment where questioning, listening, and reflecting on our own experiences and ways of knowing help us understand ourselves, each other, and the world in new ways. Once spaces have been created that encourage us to engage with difference, as Biesta (2010) insists, that engagement should be ongoing and continual. Rather than an isolated, dramatic, individual episode, this ought to be a step toward the development of a critical, artistic disposition that prizes learning, interwoven with and emerging from students' lived contexts and experiences (Martin et al., 2007). My hope is that this chapter is seen as one possible manifestation of the larger themes addressed and represented in this book. Further, I hope that it provokes questions and notions of musical and creative possibilities for continuing conversations and exploring relationships beyond the bounds of a singular project.[2]

5
Educating for Intelligent Belief or Unbelief

> In this new, turbulent international globalised landscape, a central
> message must be heralded: peace is more than the absence of war, it
> is living together with our differences—of sex, race, language, religion
> or culture—while furthering universal respect for justice and human
> rights on which such coexistence depends. Therefore, peace should
> never be taken for granted. It is an on-going process, a long-term goal
> which requires constant engineering, vigilance and active participa-
> tion by all individuals. It is a choice to be made on each situation, an
> everyday life decision to engage in sincere dialogue with other indi-
> vidual and communities, whether they live a block or a click away.
>
> **(UNESCO, n.d.a, para. 2)**

My go-to wish when I would blow out birthday candles or the wish I would
make at the appearance of the first star in the night sky always used to be for
world peace. I wish for world peace. But one day in class, after singing "Star
Light, Star Bright" and urging everyone to wish for world peace, a student
raised their hand and said, "Professor, what if your world peace is different
from mine?" Indeed. What if?

I write the opening of this chapter knowing, without hesitation, that in
many ways, this is the most important chapter in this book. It is most defi-
nitely the most challenging to enter, which is why I kept putting off writing
it until the end, hoping that a clear way forward would magically present itself. I had a sense that I didn't want this to be another chapter about the ins
and outs of introducing religious music into performances, a topic that has
been addressed at length in several places (National Association for Music
Education in particular) and by particular authors (see the references section
for the work of William Perrine). I also had a sense that prescribing lesson

Music and Social Justice. Cathy Benedict, Oxford University Press (2021). © Oxford University Press.
DOI: 10.1093/oso/9780190062125.003.0006.

plans would require a balancing act that might serve in the end to dismantle all of the points I have attempted to make thus far concerning dialogue.

But what I did know with clarity, and what drove the initial conception of this chapter, is that I had to begin with the following: we just do not talk about religion and faith-based traditions.

In general, we have been fairly well schooled to recognize issues such as race, gender, even socioeconomics, as socially just topics. But when it comes to speaking about religions, those of us who live and teach in a secularized democratic state have learned that while state mandates may sanction talking about religion, we are frightened to death of causing any kind of uproar; we exhibit what Woodford (2014) has described as a "pathological fear of controversy" (p. 25).

However, to ignore the fact that our students may hold values that are incommensurate with our own and with those of others is to do so, not just at our own peril but at the peril of this world. And while many values are incommensurable, there is none more so than how one comes to know the world through belief traditions and systems. I am suggesting, then, as we wrap our thinking around socially just engagements, that there is nothing more perilous than avoiding, remaining blind to, silencing, or disregarding the religious beliefs or even unbeliefs of our students. And yet it seems that the definition of a good citizen educator in a democratic state is either to tolerate or to remain blind to religious beliefs. Both, one could argue, are problematic without a more nuanced reckoning.

Secularism in democratic states has historically relied on systems of tolerance to further spaces of inclusion, operating under the assumption that "secularism generates tolerance as mutual respect among religions" (Brown, 2012, p. 7). However, the assumption that tolerance would be both read and enacted as mutual respect relies more on blind faith than on a civic responsibility to interrogate policies for which the intent might be to dissuade and dismantle pluralism. As such, I seek to embrace what might be conflicting points of view. First, "the promise of toleration is that coexistence in disagreement is possible" (Forst, 2013, p. 1), and tolerance is "an attitude that is intermediate between wholehearted acceptance and unrestrained opposition" (Scanlon, 2003, p 187). However, that said, I also enter an understanding of tolerance as one that "does not share power, extend equality, grant legitimacy or enfranchise" (Brown, 2012, p. 7). Tolerance, then, must be learning to exist in dialogue, the kind of dialogue to which I have been referring throughout this book; the kind that extends equality, realizes agency and legitimacy; the kind that has no "winners"; the kind, as Biesta (2018) writes, that is "an ongoing, lifelong challenge to exist with what and how is other; [it] is the challenge to exist as subject in the world" (p. 16).

To that end, I am driven by the demand "to think about education against prejudice in all of its forms" (Tate, 2017, p. 86) and urge "the need to find a means of communication across the chasm of belief and unbelief" (Noddings, 2008, p. 370). Hence, the purpose of this chapter is not a historical accounting of tolerance or, as I wrote, to argue for the inclusion of religious musics in the music program. Rather, just as I have in the other chapters, I take seriously Nel Noddings's "means" as a pedagogical mandate that supersedes any content or repertoire we choose to program and perform. And while this chapter may seem heavy with text, a further accounting and deeper engagement with the issues presented here are well within the reach of all educators.

Thus, I argue that whether our governmental mandates "allow" or do not "allow," we need to address the ways in which our pedagogy, our being with others, recognizes and welcomes all forms of diversity so that state-sanctioned and -mandated tolerance does not "[co-opt] our practices" (Schmidt, 2017, p. 162) to such an extent that we use these mandates "as simplistic solutions to problems with the mere intent of skirting them" (p. 163).

This is not to say that music education as a discipline has not crafted spaces that have the stamp of officially sanctioned socially just topics that serve to disrupt. Discussions linked to colonialism, gender, race, and racism, for instance, are officially welcomed. Less so are those linked to class, and yet even less so, if at all, are those linked to religion. While no one challenges the interrogation of color-blind or even gender-blind practices, we are frozen when it comes to religion. Thus, even when confronted with visible markings of religious belief systems, we tend to engage in religion-blind "common-sense" engagements. This logic, however, is similar to color-blind practices. If teachers treat all students as if they are the same, "[that usually means] that their model of the ideal student is white and middle-class and that all students are treated as if they are or should be both white and middle-class" (Irvine, 1991, p. 54). Just so in religion-blind practices. In secular democracies, particularly the United States, by ignoring the belief (and unbelief) traditions and systems of our students, we tend to treat students as if everyone is or should fall somewhere on a broad spectrum of Christianity or, in our more aware moments (in certain parts of North America), Jewish traditions.

We reside now in the midst of a perfect storm, the nexus between ideologies of politics, class, race, and religion. Sitting out the storm (or, worse, allowing ourselves to be frightened by the storm) and tiptoeing one's way tentatively through accountability and "hyper-punitive policies and practices" (Giroux,

2017, p. 2) feels like common sense. Surrendering to preserving this particular common-sense view of how the world functions, however, means abandoning disruptive pedagogies. Disruptive in this case need not be read as a complete dismantling of all things conservative but rather seen as a tool to "consider all perspectives," "despite divergent philosophical bases" (Perrine, 2017b, p. 7).

Implications for Music Educators

In order to further underscore these points, I turn to Nel Noddings as *the* unwavering and devoted teacher to help frame pedagogical possibilities. Noddings (1993), forever stalwart and fueled by the mind of both a mathematician and a philosopher, has for a very long time recognized the paralyzing effects ignoring religion has had on students. Never one to shy away from the ethical heart of an issue, she declares, "it would be morally reprehensible" not to discuss "controversial moral issues" and that we "must be prepared" to do so (p. 123). Educating for intelligent belief or unbelief, as Noddings suggests, means taking on a pedagogy of neutrality, which for her does not mean the neutrality of silence, which in itself is unneutral. Rather, just as we grapple with critical race theory and language that embraces gender-identity fluidity in our classrooms, we must extend those practices toward belief and unbelief systems. I have observed Noddings teaching, and this is not simply the affordance of a space where ideas and stories are tossed about. She is a master at listening and insists that an "obligation to present all significant sides of an issue in their full passion" must also be driven by "best reasoning" (p. 12). "Students," she writes, "must be allowed, even encouraged to ask how, why, and on what grounds" (p. 123). In order to do this, however, students must learn communication skills that move them beyond simply agreeing and disagreeing and even consensus.[1] In order to learn to ask how, why, and on what grounds, students must also be taught the skills of reflexivity in order to recognize the ways in which their subjectivity (including belief and unbelief traditions) influences their reasoning (Fook, 1999), so that they can become more aware "of the sociopolitical circumstances and individual preconceptions that surround and influence [them] to act in particular ways" (Ocádiz Velázquez, 2020).

In terms of religion, this is, of course, easier said than done, particularly with younger students. And while Noddings (2008) recognizes that many of her suggestions fall in the realm of "theoretical possibilities" (p. 370), I believe it is possible in practice to create spaces of critical recognition, just as we do when addressing gender and race. The issue, though, is not simply to argue for the inclusion of religious musics in the school curriculum. Nor is it to argue for extensive program notes, which is one of the ways US teachers can demonstrate that the inclusions of these musics is worthy of study. In fact, I would argue that relying on each of these methods as a way to address and acknowledge religion (and more often than not, these musics are a representation of Christianity) simply underscores my arguments: treating any piece of music simply in terms of instrumental ends (particularly the musics presented in this chapter) is to silence the ways in which belief systems of all kinds have influenced and shaped creative engagements throughout time.

Pedagogical Implications

Educators, as Christopher Knaus (2009) writes, "must remember how students live before, during and after school. To fail to consider students' personal context is to ensure that what we teach is irrelevant to their daily survival" (p. 139). If we remain silent to the belief and unbelief traditions and systems of our students, we may be creating the "impression in the minds of the young that religion is unimportant and has nothing to contribute to the solution of the perennial and ultimate problems of human life" (American Council on Education, 1953, p. 6). It is also to deprive them and ourselves of the possibility of turning an interrogative eye toward all belief systems. Unfortunately, as Noddings (2008) points out, when religion *is* talked about in schools, more often than not, "[teachers] avoid the critical discussion of beliefs and refer to (for instance) religious wars and persecutions with delicacy, often treating them as anomalies" (p. 370). While war may not play a role in our discussions with students, surely it ought to. Throughout history, regimes of war have banned cultural practices linked to music. For instance, the Taliban in Afghanistan outlawed playing or listening to music by anyone, further repressing women's rights who were no longer allowed to sing to their children in the home. And of course, issues such as what dominant religious power or personage paid for musics to be composed, for what purposes they were intended, what toll this may have taken on composers, and in what ways religious affordance allowed certain musics to move through time while others remained ignored and erased must be part of our conversations with students.

I recognize, then, as does Bouma (2017), that how we choose to focus dialogue frames directional ends. For instance, if classroom conversations frame "belief and creed, arguments," conversations tend to gravitate toward discussing "what is correct and what is not" (p. 130). However, providing space that helps students to "encounter the religious 'other' " in their day-to-day lived experience allows for a differing kind of dialogue, dialogue that is "designed to promote intergroup understanding and respect both among groups and individuals" (p. 129). It is helpful, thus, to consider Noddings's thinking on pedagogical neutrality much as we would when we apply the tenets of critical race theory. Critical race theory demands of us that we provide the space for "counterstorytelling" (Delgado, 2013) or narratives "that [aim] to subvert or interrupt the dominant narrative" (Hess, 2019, p. 4). And while the following pedagogical strategies may appear simplistic, I view them as not, as they interrupt the dominant narrative of religion-blindness and move us from the "morally reprehensible" realm into the moral influence realm of vocation (Hansen, 1994). Hansen (1993) suggests that while there may not be a direct "cause and effect, at least not in any direct or easily measurable sense" (p. 398), we can and do "invite" students through our moral influence in ways that underscore our "often tacit, standards and expectations" (p. 397). We wield an awful lot of power. How we choose to view the construction and flow of this power and the "enduring influence [this has on our] students" calls us to attend more mindfully to "that which we least attend" (p. 398).

First of all, I firmly believe that we must make explicit to our students our pedagogical goals and not simply hope that they intuit them. Thus, the first place I begin is to talk with students about the importance of addressing social justice education by thinking through—together—issues of race, socioeconomics, gender constructions and fluidity, and religion. Saying these words out loud signals to students that I will not shy away from bringing these issues forward; I will note these issues as they arise and, perhaps more important, name them when they are not being named. Second, I have started to purposefully attend to religious or religiously grounded comments from students in ways that I would have covered up and brushed aside in the past. For instance, at the elementary level, a student recently recounted a story about engaging with a homeless man who ended up teaching him more than he had expected and how thankful he was that he stopped to engage with this man. While there were many ways I could have responded, not least among them to facilely treat the story as a lesson well learned, I purposefully remarked, "Oh, this sounds similar to various religious parables and creation stories I have read." On another occasion, I was addressing how to take notes in such a way that helps situate oneself reflexively and told the class, "I do this all the time. If I find myself in a house of worship, for instance, I am the kind of person who takes notes on the back of the 'program' so that I can continue to think about issues that have been raised." Across grades, I encourage projects that connect students with the musics they hear in all parts of their worlds, including houses of worship, thus actively encouraging students to share their faith-based traditions of knowing the world as much as I encourage them to share with the class the kinds of musics to which they gravitate. In a musicianship class, I wonder with students whether solfège covers of Christmas carols is indoctrinating and in that same class let them know that when it comes time for the midterm and final projects, covering religious music is absolutely acceptable. What I have discovered in these shifts I have actively made reaffirms my belief in the ethical imperative behind these momentary, but public, connections. Several students have approached me and expressed thanks for the public affordance of personal religious identity. They share that throughout their schooling, they have had to keep this part of themselves hidden and covered. In these moments, I understand and live the teachings of both Martin Buber and Hannah Arendt. Not only am I able to "pause," as Tate (2017) writes, to "explore further the implications of difficult situations, see things from different angles and refine [my] judgment" (p. 188), but I believe students are able to do so as well. Indeed, I believe that in all of these pedagogical moments where space is afforded for epistemological humility, my being feels most alive and aware with the other (Buber, 1947/2003).

Curricular Implications

How students come to know their world through and with our teaching should be an integral step toward preparing students to live in a world, as Noddings (2008) writes, of "pluralistic values" (p. 386). Perhaps I have become more aware of this while living in Canada these past five years, where epistemological frameworks that recognize and bring mindfully into the curriculum Indigenous ways of knowing demand morally essential and ethical beginning points. I am heartened when I read of the Denver public school system in Colorado revisiting its curriculum to interrogate the "myths and untruths" surrounding Native American peoples (Asmar, 2019, para. 12). These moments call me to recognize the startling veracity in the words of Noddings (2008) when she reminds us that

> Religion plays a significant role in the lives of individuals, and increasingly it is playing a political role that affects both believers and unbelievers. We cannot remain silent on this vital topic and still claim to educate. (p. 386)

What, then, will this look like in an upper-primary/middle-school context? Rather than articulating specific lesson plans, as I have done in other chapters, here I outline possible unit ideas that might be brought into the upper-primary (Canada, fourth to eighth grade) and middle-school through high school environments. Again, at the heart of this chapter is the idea that diversity and pluralism begin in dialogue. While in previous chapters I have outlined specific ways of going about scaffolding dialogue and discussion in music classrooms, I turn in this chapter to UNESCO and its use of intercultural dialogue:

> Intercultural dialogue specifically refers to dialogues occurring between members of different cultural groups. Intercultural dialogue assumes that participants agree to listen to and understand multiple perspectives, including even those held by groups or individuals with whom they disagree. (UNESCO, n.d.b)

Intercultural dialogue opens up the space for the interrogation of words and terms (as we have done throughout the opening chapters) to help students think through assumptions they may bring to belief and unbelief practices. For instance, placing the word *religion* as the beginning point of a thinking map could very well reveal and uncover misunderstandings and biases that open further space for dialogue. However, I am acutely aware and respectful of faith-based practices that simply do not allow for introspection and interrogation. Thus, I am cognizant of the tightrope one must walk in preserving the belief and unbelief understandings young students bring to public schooling that are rooted in familial and cultural understandings and ways of being. But rather than seeing this as another manifestation of "[being fearful] of controversy" (Woodford, 2014, p. 25), I interpret recognition and dialogue as consistent with UNESCO's goal of "[promoting] interreligious understanding and respect" in order "to achieve the aims of enhancing mutual respect and decreasing intergroup tension and peace" (Bouma, 2017, p. 130).

As a US citizen who moved to Canada at the same time the Truth and Reconciliation Commission of Canada published its findings and calls to action (2015), I have become keenly aware of the deep harm and damage religious indoctrination did to generations of Indigenous peoples. Similar to atrocities done throughout time that have been justified by representatives of religious faiths and reigning governments, young children throughout Canada were forcibly taken from their homes and placed in residential schools so as to integrate them into a dominant vision of Canadian society. Attending to such atrocities with young students (through the lens of colonialization) is a mandate of the British Columbia curriculum (and soon to be made manifest as other provinces renew their provincial curricula). Clearly, conversations that articulate religious purging may not translate neatly into other forms of extreme indoctrination, but as a provincially mandated curricular competency, the entry point exists as one to be taken advantage of.

Surely more of these entry points exist in ways we have just not been able to see. Indeed, entry points might also come in the guise of "essential questions." Many of us work in boards and districts where essential questions are used to both frame our music curriculum and connect it to other disciplines. The following are only a few that afford a justified way forward:

How do individuals develop values and beliefs?

What factors shape our values and beliefs?

How do values and beliefs change over time?

How are belief systems represented and reproduced through history, literature, art, and music?

What happens when belief systems of societies and individuals come into conflict? (TeachThought, 2018)

Once we are better able to open ourselves to how these issues might be addressed in ways that continue to honor mandates of separation of church and state, we can deliberately plan for them. After much consideration, then, about what I could offer in terms of concrete suggestions, I settled on chants and chanting as a way to open the space for both spoken and musical dialogue. One reason I do so is that children from a very young age understand the power and place of chanting in and throughout their lives. Thus, in the following section, I first present a curricular rationale grounded in the educational work of the US Freedom Forum First Amendment Center, followed by a broad overview of a unit that focuses on chants and chanting. I then finish with suggestions for other possible units. As in other chapters, the goal here is not to compare and contrast in order to decide that one is better than the other but rather to think through multiple ways of knowing the world as we celebrate and embrace difference.

Chants and Chanting

The US Freedom Forum First Amendment Center has published a document titled *Living with Our Deepest Differences: Religious Liberty in a Pluralistic Society* (Freedom Forum Institute, 2009). This center is particularly focused on what can and cannot be included in US public schools when attending to the First Amendment to the Constitution.[2] Thus, in this document, much care and attention have been paid to teaching *about* religion and the possibilities therein. The authors present several possible units, including one that focuses on "the 'for better, for worse' consequences of leaving diverse faiths free to enter public life" (p. 117). The purpose of the unit is to help students think through current debates being played out in the media, with the goal of having them "think through how these experiences would have been different without religious liberty and the pioneers of ideas and laws who made it possible" (p. 118). The authors frame this discussion by posing such questions as "What is the impact of things such as music, slogans and flags in cementing [solidarities found in 'tribes']?" (p. 118). While the unit is focused particularly on "Protestant and Catholic tribes" in Ulster, a music teacher certainly could extend this idea to multiple cultures in which music has been used to trouble, rally, or (in short) impact religious sentiment.[3]

There are also other curricular ideas throughout the pamphlet that, while not specifically musical, could be translated into more musical applications, including one that focuses on religious liberty (pp. 80–81), a unit that would facilitate powerful interdisciplinary engagements. Considering that all of public life (not just "American") is pluralistic in all its manifestations, including religion, this unit, while focusing solely on the role of religious liberty in public life (p. 70), provides a rationale for the creation of other units, including one that would address musical chants and chanting.

While there are multiple sources to help teachers think through framing chant, Caryn Neumann (2006) defines chant the following way:

Chanting is a type of sung speech that is used to quiet the mind and body or to aid in memorization. The book-focused religions of Christianity, Judaism, and Islam include chanting as part of worship, but the practice is more heavily used in animistic and Eastern religions, especially Buddhism. (p. 68)

In her chapter, Neumann points out that chanting can be traced back to prehistoric peoples who used "shamans to mediate between the visible and spirit worlds" (p. 68). She then follows a progress of chant that originates in Greece, moves into Eastern religions, and then moves into the West with Gregorian chant. Of course, chant also opens up pathways into Indigenous cultures as a way of preserving culture and as a way of knowing and encountering "different natural and social spheres" (Diamond, 2008, p. 3). However, with whom, for whom, and for what purpose these encounters are intended remain constant questions for all of us concerned with social justice and socially just engagements.

Here, of course, is the issue with chants: precisely because of the way they are often used as a memorization device and as a way to "enhance emotional excitation" (Neumann, 2006, p. 68), it may be that singing and performing some of these could trigger indoctrination concerns. Thus, when one is teaching in contexts where singing these kinds of musics may be seen as an infringement upon state-mandated rights, care must be taken to address these issues frankly with students and even principals and parents. Finding and humming the pedal point is one way to enter the music, as is singing the melodies on neutral syllables. However, it is imperative to understand that treating the chants this way may denigrate and even colonize musics that were meant for very specific purposes. Of particular concern are musics from Indigenous cultures, always presented through the relational (often as a gift) and always through story. These components are not just integral to the music, but they constitute in their completeness a way of honoring, knowing, and experiencing the world.

Students of all ages can grapple with conversations in which the teacher addresses their worlds and their ways of knowing. Just as I articulated possible moments of purposefully attending to religious or religiously grounded comments, teachers must not shirk or abandon open dialogue about state-mandated objectives that exist (at least in the United States) to both respect and make free public expressions of religious beliefs.

Unit Description

Prior to deciding which chants to use, consider how deeply you want to delve into the historical/political dimensions. Indeed, this kind of project might work best as a student (individual or group) research project. However, keep in mind that the way in which the background to these musics is presented, particularly with those from and of Indigenous peoples, again, is integral to the musics themselves. Most, if not all, of the musics I am suggesting are passed down through the oral tradition, certainly a way of presenting that is familiar to elementary music teachers. However, and this is a *big* however, the oral tradition in Indigenous cultures and others *is* a way of knowing:

> Furthermore, [many Indigenous teachers] stress that knowledge and ways of knowing are impossible to distinguish. The process of transmission is part of the knowledge itself. (Diamond, 2008, p. 9)

In other words, there is a big difference between rote teaching a song so that it can then be used for another purpose versus encountering these musics as ways of knowing and as traditional Indigenous knowledge. You can imagine, then, that a PowerPoint presentation with the purpose of "teaching" (with the ultimate goal of testing that knowledge) is problematic. Equally as problematic is notating these musics with the goal of pulling musical elements from them in order to teach Western notation! Thus, one way to acknowledge these issues is to come to know your Indigenous community, attend Pow Wows and invite elders and other religious representatives from the community into the classroom.

Chants from Around Our World

The following are suggestions of possible musics to incorporate into the classroom. In terms of the historical presentation of these chants, the goal in this chapter is to introduce the musics themselves. Students could be the ones to research the historical contexts.

Indigenous musics. As with other musics, it is almost impossible to select one area for study here. However, and more important, when encountering Indigenous musics, one must again recognize that many songs must be gifted in order to be taught and performed. Not appropriating these musics, and understanding the transmission history, then, must be first and foremost in one's mind when considering resources to include. Ideally, it would be best to work with nearby Indigenous, First Nations/Peoples, and Native American communities. There are multiple sources, however, to which one can turn. In particular, the Truth and Reconciliation Commission of Canada (2015) has published many materials that help frame the educative process.[4]

Greek Orthodox Byzantine chants. Keep in mind that these chants are still relevant today for students who may attend and worship in a Greek Orthodox church.[5]

Islamic chants. In a unit that addresses chant in religious contexts, it is imperative to include Islamic music. I am aware that this is a point where teachers may draw the line, but this is exactly where the line should not be drawn. In Canada, where I now live, Muslim students from all over the world populate all levels of

> This might be a good time to remind readers not to put students on the spot. Do not assume that simply because students attend a particular faith-based house of worship (for instance), they can speak to the musical practices within.

schooling. And whether we realize it or not, this is the same all over the world. The problematic reasons we may be unaware of have to do with laws and a rising xenophobia permeating all areas of our lives. The laws, more often than not, purport to be grounded in the separation of church and state and religious neutrality. One such example in Canada is Bill 21, recently passed in Quebec, banning the wearing of religious symbols for public employees, including school principals, vice principals, and teachers[6] These are laws that students should be aware of, as religious symbols also include jewelry that can be seen.[7] I contend that the music classroom can be a place where dialogue centering around all peoples in and through their music not only belongs but should be welcomed, embraced, and celebrated.

Of course, as with all cultures, there isn't such a thing as a monolithic Muslim culture, and for certain, there isn't such a thing as one kind of Islamic music. These are points that *must* be underscored. The goal is to frame these musical engagements so that students move beyond (if they need to move beyond) a unilateral extreme vision of Islam and Islamic ways of knowing the world. The challenge (there will be several challenges) is not to trivialize the musics you do choose. For instance, in choosing Sufi music, where you could focus on the chants that are inextricably intertwined with rhythmic dancing, you would not want to trivialize the whirling movements as simply a dance; they are a remembrance of God.[8]

Chants of South Asia—Hinduism. Note that all of the points addressed above are applicable here as well; there are many musics in and originating in South Asia. You can use (for instance) *Chants of India* by Ravi Shankar (produced by and with contributions from George Harrison) as an example of Vedic and other Hindu sacred prayers set to music.[9]

Gregorian chants. There are many recordings of Gregorian chants:

- The Benedictine monks of Santo Domingo de Silos, produced *The Best of Gregorian Chants*, which earned them one platinum and two gold discs in 1994. Check out Giles (1994) to read how the monks responded to the overwhelming press coverage they received: "You have to understand, we are monks, not rock stars."
- Include examples from Saint Hildegard of Bingen (1098–1179). In what ways do her compositions differ from those by male composers? Why might that be? Why are there not more examples of female composers?
- Include chants produced and sung by women; have students make note of the differences and similarities to those sung by male voices.
- Incorporate, for instance, the documentary *Work & Pray: Living the Psalms with the Nuns of Regina Laudis* and the recording *Women in Chant: Gregorian Chants for the Festal Celebrations of the Virgin Martyrs and Our Lady of Sorrows.*

Other engagements with chants:

- The Bee Gees' "Every Christian Lion Hearted Man Will Show You" (1967) begins with and uses chant throughout as a compositional device.

- In "Blackstar" (2016), David Bowie uses chant as a device that is almost tone-cluster-like in quality. The song also appears on the last album he recorded before passing away.
- Brittany Howard recently recorded a spoken word piece entitled "13th Century Metal" (2019). She describes the composition as follows: "The chords are very Gregorian, but it's also metal—it's got rage in it" (Petruish, para 22). This is a powerful piece; these chords not only recall elements of chant but frame her thinking on issues of "love, compassion, and humanity," as well as opposition to "those whose will is to divide us / And who are determined to keep us in the dark ages of fear."

There are more, but for those of you interested in using chant as a compositional device, check out the Benzedrine Monks of Santo Domonica (clearly a spin on the aforementioned Benedictine monks of Santo Domingo de Silos). They cover popular music such as "We Will Rock You," "Smells Like Teen Spirit," and the theme from *The Monkees*.[10]

Guiding Questions for Research Projects

The following guiding questions can frame the unit from the perspective of either the teacher's or the students' research:

1. Determine the purpose of each chant. How and why did they originate?
2. Determine the compositional style (time period, the significance of the use of modes and which modes, melodic contour, rhythms, etc.).
3. Determine who was/is allowed to sing and perform the chants and why this was/is so.
4. Which style do you personally prefer? Is one more effective than another? Effective at what?
5. In what ways were those chants influenced by musics that came before?
6. What are current examples from today? In what ways have they changed or stayed the same?
7. Are chantlike melodies found in popular music? To what end and purpose do you think the composers used them? Are there any religious implications for appropriating styles of music?
8. Compose or cover your own chant.

Other Possible Unit Ideas

Music as weapon. Chant is only one way to link musicking to faith-based ways of knowing the world. Addressing how music has been used politically throughout time is one way to help students understand that music has also been "used as torture by American troops during the second War in Iraq, or as an incitement to genocide in the Rwandan crisis of 1994" (Woodford, 2014, p. 33). Suzanne Cusick (2006) has written an article addressing the ways in which music has been used as an acoustic weapon of no-touch torture, including sonic blasts, "in the interrogation of Iraqi detainees, playing the songs repeatedly at high volume inside of shipping containers" (para. 9), and musics that would be found religiously offensive. Certainly, the point could be made that playing Barney the big purple dinosaur's song "I Love You, You Love Me" over and over and over to hostages who would find this music vile is a corrupt use of chant. These are not easy ideas to embrace, particularly when music often plays such an uplifting role in our lives. But these are exactly the kinds of issues that speak to students on a personal level and encourage them to think critically about something assumed as universally good.

Rites of initiation and passage. Music teachers can plan a unit addressing the role music plays in celebratory rites of initiation and passage, including (for instance) coming of age, unions, death, and birth. This could be a way to welcome in the individual practices of the students in your classrooms and study *about* the music in these rites.

Carnival. The role music plays in the celebration of Carnival opens up spaces to address musical practices in (among others) Trinidad, Brazil, Spain, New Orleans, and Grenada.[11] Such a unit could speak to the ways in which cultures engage with celebrating pre-Lent and how those practices have emerged and have been represented in distinct practices, often influencing other musical paths.

Lingering Issues

> Religious differences do exist. Rather than a deemphasis of differences (and similarities), the school has the ecumenical obligation and Constitutional right to study these. (Schwadron, 1970, p. 164)

I am always already a stranger to the other—at least, I hope to be. Particularly in the ways Arendt sees the possibilities of distance and strangerhood. Phillip Hansen (2004), in thinking through Arendt's conception of strangerhood, reminds us that

> To be a stranger is to exist for others prior to the ascription of value; or to relate to others without indifference, hostility or beneficence. But it is to have an identity, to confront others as a person, and this creates "space" in which to appear. (p. 7)

I wrestle with these implications; I know I fail daily at the task that Hansen, Biesta, Buber, Arendt, and others place before me. I also struggle with the existential doom that seems to pervade every area of our lives, particularly policies whose mode of rationality (such as neoliberal, authoritarian, and populist) extends their governance in ways that suggest the "good for" or common sense. Giroux (2018) asks us to "make education central to politics that changes the way people think, desire, hope and act" (p. 11). Education may be central to dismantling or at least interrogating these modes, but education, thus presented, must be inextricably linked to deliberate pedagogical engagements. I am not yet quite able to give up wishing for world peace, but as I become more mindful of incommensurate ways of being, I now work toward a conception of peace that calls me to attend to the other prior to the ascription of value, to deliberately model the moral influence of a pause that creates the space for appearance. In order to do this, I must recognize the belief and unbelief ways of knowing the world that my students hold and realize that whether or not they are commensurable with mine is not the issue. The issue is to come to better understandings of how we come to know the world and to celebrate and honor difference.

6
Politics of Song

Throughout this book, there has been an implied assumption that music, in all presentations (whether we are listening to a story that speaks of music in the lives of others or listening and performing), can lead toward the heightened awareness of social inequities. But this does not happen magically. Just as reading stories about bullying doesn't prevent bullying, listening to music doesn't enact social transformation. Indeed, experiencing music (mediated by others and/or through technology) "can easily be a *diversion* from political and movement activity rather than an aid" (Rosenthal & Flacks, 2011, p. 183; emphasis in original). This is certainly not a new argument, and it was most infamously made by Theodor Adorno in 1941 in his essay "On Popular Music," where he suggests (among other things) that "the tunes themselves lull the listener to inattention. They tell him not to worry for he will not miss anything" (para. 35). While this essay has been delved into and interrogated since it was published, I do, however, have something of the same concern that stems from an experience I once had listening to Madonna's "Holiday" (1983). As I was singing along, I realized that what she was suggesting was that the solution to the world's most complex problems could be "turn[ed] around" if we all simply took a holiday and celebrated. This music was essentially functioning as a slogan, not just an empty slogan but one I felt to be dangerous for the same reasons Adorno articulated. Not only had I been lulled to inattention as I sang along with the harmony line attached to the lyric "It would be so nice," but it also felt as if I was doing something about the problems of the world simply by singing along! I realize I am presenting a complex argument in simple terms, and agree with Rosenthal and Flacks (2011) when they point out that "the uses, functions, and effects of music in movements are surprisingly and intriguingly complicated" (p. 4). This is why I have been arguing for pedagogical encounters that provide for interrogative discussions. We need to think through all of these complexities with students so that they begin to attend.

Music and Social Justice. Cathy Benedict, Oxford University Press (2021). © Oxford University Press.
DOI: 10.1093/oso/9780190062125.003.0007.

Looking at song as political action is not the same as bringing politics into the classroom. The latter is about ideological positioning, and the first is coming to understand how music and songs come from the world and go back into the world. People use songs, and they are mediated by songs. Music shapes society, and society is shaped by music and musicking. Elementary students are more than able to grapple with concepts such as identity construction and representation in song. Music as protest, propaganda, and resistance (Street, 2017) is also well within their cognitive, if not visceral, understanding. *Political* in this context, then, is how we place ourselves in the world and what we hope for ourselves and those around us, not as a universal but as a commitment to daily living with and among others. Education in its broadest sense is about the formation of the social being in a pluralist context. Particularly in this time of hyper-individualism, schooling must reach beyond the individual child, for as John Dewey (1907) reminds us, "any other ideal for our schools is narrow and unlovely; acted upon, it destroys our democracy" (p. 19).

Who isn't drawn to the use of music as a form of protest? Music has always been used this way: music is mobile, it is slippery in its quickness and ubiquity, and now it can travel anywhere and everywhere at the click of a mouse. The "lyrics, like poetry, allow for meaning to be hinted at, rather than stated explicitly" (Street, 2017, p. 3), thus making it difficult for an offending power to surveil and punish. As a form of "bearing-witness" (p. 3), music used in this way is clearly understood as a form of political action. Thinking about music as propaganda reminds us of the way music can be used to further agendas. Political parties have always used music to send messages; as they choose music to be played as they walk on and off stage at official appearances, for instance. Two issues to contemplate, however, become apparent. First, the artists are often not pleased, as they see the use of their music as a tacit sign of their approval of the party. Second, the messages embedded in the texts themselves often conflict with the intended message of the political party. For instance, when Ronald Reagan was running for president, he used Bruce Springsteen's "Born in the U.S.A." to walk onto the stage. However, as Dewberry and Millen (2014) point out, "Upon looking beyond the chorus, 'Born in the U.S.A.' portrays an American dream gone awry, which ran against Reagan's Republican conservatism persona" (p. 82). What fascinating questions, then, to pose with students: *How is it that musics get used the way they get used? What is the purpose of music? What happens to the original intent and vision of the artist once the music is let go into the world? And most significantly for this chapter, what happens to musics that were intended for a socially driven purpose but become used in ways that undermine their previous social significance? What does it mean to listen with an activist's stance?*

"Imagine" by John Lennon (Grades 5–8 and Higher)

Music is more than an object of study: it is a way of perceiving the world. A tool for understanding. (Attali, 1985, p. 4)

One might argue that the ubiquity of John Lennon's "Imagine" is such that, as Randall Allsup (2011) suggests, "we can no longer hear [it] in new or interesting ways" (p. 32). When we do hear it, we may hum along and sing a few lyrics here and there and perhaps even recount that there is some kind of issue in the song that got Lennon in trouble, and what about that Yoko, who did she think she was, anyway? and on and on. But are we able to encounter this music in dialogue? And once we do take time to hear and be with this music anew (or, for many of our students, for the first time) and realize the countless times and ways this music has been covered or sampled, do we wonder if its trajectory could have possibly been predicted by Lennon? Could the trajectory even have been desired by Lennon?

These questions of desire and trajectory reside at the heart of these lessons: for whom, for what purpose, at what cost.

The genesis of the following set of plans emerged from that same 2011 article in which Allsup outlines a lesson geared toward helping students hear in "new or interesting ways" (p. 32). He does so by introducing the music (without telling students what he is playing) by vamping the first two chords of the song. After the chords settle in the ears of the students, he motions for them to join in, improvising in and with these two chords. After a time, and after they have settled into the groove, he plays "Imagine," which then prompts the class into discussion:

The class discussion shifts away from music (or has it?) toward the strong emotional memories attached to this song, as well as to the problems of the world, of politics and social justice. The classroom space becomes electrically charged: intimate, angry, revelatory, even radical. (Allsup, 2011, p. 32)

As an elementary teacher with an Orff certification, I immediately saw the possibilities in this, as the two opening chords fit well on the barred instruments. But then I began thinking about how many times this music has been covered and what that might mean for pushing further into Lennon's message. I also realized, as I listened to multiple covers of "Imagine," how his original message not only had stayed with us but has taken on more immediacy. In 2014, I was contracted by the Kennedy Center's Changing Education Through the Arts Program[1] to present to local Washington, D.C., teachers a unit to support the goals of the YoungArts MasterClass study guide.[2] I chose Lennon's "Imagine" as one of my master texts. After working with several of the cover versions that I felt stayed true to Lennon's message, I also chose to include Cisco's commercial that uses "Imagine" in order to sell its products.

I took the lessons into five Miami-Dade County, Florida, schools and worked with five different groups of middle-school teachers and students. Many of the schools were in underserved communities, steeped in confounding issues that often left the teachers feeling they had to be in control of every moment. This was the first time I heard comments such as "I was *surprised* by how involved they were and what they had to say . . . students who never participated were now engaging." I remember being shaken up by these comments. Here were teachers who had volunteered to be part of this project, thus more than likely engaged with their students in deep ways, and yet who also admitted that they had been unwilling to let go, to teach the way they wanted to teach, the way they knew they should be teaching. It was in Miami that I realized students were not just able but hungry to address issues such as religion, racism, and poverty. I never once had an issue with conversations centering around Lennon's text; students knew exactly what he meant when he sang:

> Imagine there's no heaven
> It's easy if you try
> No hell below us
> Above us only sky

I knew then the possibilities of dialogue and what that would mean for teachers who were willing to see their students differently.

Fast-forward to 2019, when I had the opportunity to teach this unit in two different contexts. The first was at the October Nova Scotia Music Educators Association (NSMEA) conference. In remarkable support of their teachers, the Nova Scotia school board provides a professional development day to every teacher. NSMEA organized various sessions for the music teachers at a beautiful new middle school; I was invited to present both the *Peter and the Wolf* lesson plan (chapter 2) and this "Imagine" unit. I was thankful for the opportunity, as I had not yet had the chance to ask music teachers what they thought about the feasibility of these units. Two things happened during these sessions that are worth noting. The teachers themselves loved the opportunity to listen critically and think and engage with the people near them. They loved immersing themselves in a piece of music they probably had not visited in depth for some time—and for many new teachers, perhaps ever. And many of them took the plan back to their classrooms, assuring me that they would let me know how their students responded. Again, the comments I received were about how surprised they were that their students were able to dialogue critically with one another and how much more intense the dialogue made the listening encounter.

The second opportunity came with the same music teacher who had allowed me to work with her second- and third-grade class on the lullaby unit (chapter 1) and friendship and bullying unit (chapter 3). I presented the "Imagine" unit to her fifth- and sixth-grade classes over two class periods (although three class periods would have been ideal). As I was able to teach two different classes of fifth- and sixth-graders, I was also able to fine-tune the lessons. One thing I noticed with the first class was that they were having challenges speaking to the person nearest them. So in the second class, when it came time to discuss, I got them out of the three rows they had been sitting in and had them move around and chat with someone new. This forced them to listen and respond differently each time they met up with a new partner. I also noticed during the first class that after speaking with their partner, they were unwilling to share their thinking with the entire class. During the second class, then, I told them I was going to count to three, after which they were all going to yell out their thinking at the same time. This actually worked. After yelling and hearing their own thinking out loud, they were much more willing to open up to the rest of the group. Of course, these were students who had no relationship with me until I walked through their door asking them to do something no one had ever asked them to do. So just imagine the possibilities with your own students.

John Lennon's "Imagine" (1971)

Note that we can no longer assume that students know who the Beatles are; therefore, I put together a PPT presentation that situates both the Beatles and John Lennon. I included photos from when he was young, as well as a still from when he produced the video. You should also address who the woman is in the video (Yoko Ono).

TEACHER: In 1971, John Lennon (a former member of the rock group the Beatles) wrote and composed the song "Imagine." Before we talk about the lyrics, I want us to watch the video. As we watch, attend to the music and the lyrics and the ways in which the images and movement support Lennon's message.

Watch the video of "Imagine":[3] https://www.youtube.com/watch?v= VOgFZfRVaww

Post-video discussion prompts:

- What did you notice in the video? (Light, movement, stillness.)
- What about the music and the images—what did you notice? (Encourage them to discuss the music even if they are not using what they might think of as musical terms. The goal is to get them reflecting mindfully and in detail on what they saw and heard.)
- What is the message of the text?
- In what ways is that message represented in the video?

During the discussion, the issue of Lennon speaking about no heaven and no religion may come up; if it doesn't you should bring it up for them. It may help to have this quote of Lennon's ready as you speak of this phrase not as one that is literal but rather as a metaphor:

The concept of positive prayer. . . . If you can *imagine* a world at peace, with no denominations of religion—not without religion but without this my-God-is-bigger-than-your-God thing—then it can be true. . . . The World Church called me once and asked, "Can we use the lyrics to 'Imagine' and just change it to 'Imagine *one* religion'?" That showed [me] they didn't understand it at all. It would defeat the whole purpose of the song, the whole idea. (Sheff, 1981)

However, students have no difficulty in seeing the images in the video metaphorically. They often speak of Ono letting in the light and connect that to the text. They also are quite able to recognize the text as metaphorical and not literal.

Glee's Version of "Imagine" (2009)

As students are finishing up the Lennon discussion, move the conversation toward how this music has appeared over time in differing contexts—including the next one, from the TV show Glee.[4]

TEACHER: In this episode of *Glee*, kids are preparing for a competition and are feeling very full of themselves and have just finished performing an over-the-top number for the school they will be competing against. As you watch, attend to your reactions throughout the song.

Watch "Hairography" (*Glee*, season 1, episode 11): http://www.youtube.com/watch?v=cSlGocYJ2Dk

Post-video discussion prompts:

- What was your immediate reaction to the video? Share with the person next to you. (Open up to class sharing, and see my note below.)
- What were the differences you noticed?
- Has the meaning of the text shifted?
- What do you think about the *Glee* kids and their interactions with the other choir?
- What would John Lennon think of this version, and why?

This is a powerful version, as it raises many points of discussion, not least among them that the choir is a hearing-impaired choir and they are signing the lyrics. When I do this with students, I always share with them that when I first saw this video, I was shocked that the opening singer wasn't able to sing! Of course, I was horrified at my initial reaction once I figured out what was going on, but this is typically the response of many, and they appreciate me sharing that I responded similarly. One of the first things they share beyond their opening reaction is that they do not understand why the *Glee* students had to swoop in and "save" the other choir. I love that discussion, as it highlights the issue of what is considered "normal," as well as abilities and differing abilities. *What does it mean to engage with others respectfully and with humility rather than from a position of false generosity?*

Ti'Jean's Version, "Just Imagine" (2009)

You will want to situate the time frame of this video. For instance, 2009 is three years into President Obama's first term.

TEACHER: We now move to a context in which the artist Ti'Jean engages with "Imagine" by reimagining it as "Just Imagine." As you watch, keep in mind the previous two versions (Lennon and *Glee*). What do you immediately notice in Ti'Jean's version, and how does it differ from the others?

Watch Ti'Jean's video: http://www.youtube.com/watch?v=lHv6tXvybPo
Post-video discussion prompts:

- What is Ti'Jean doing?
- What is his message?
- In what ways does his interpretation differ from the other two we have watched?
- What might John Lennon feel about this interpretation, and why?

The lyrics go by very quickly in this version. The first time, I play it without handing out the lyrics and have them think through with the other what they have heard and their reactions. After the initial discussion, I pass out the lyrics and have them discuss the text in detail:

> hey yo they say that I'm a dreamer but I know I'm not the only one
> they get me through the hard times when I can't see the sun
>
> sometimes I want to run and just disappear
> imagine all my mom's tears
> imagine if I faced my fears
> my friends would do would many years
>
> wish I could set you free with the music that you hear
> imagine if we all cared
> imagine my imagination if I never stared at the beauty all around me
>   that we all share so imagine if I never wrote I never spoke my mind
> imagine if John Lennon never wrote these rhymes and
> imagine all the fellas never did those petty crimes
> the signs of the times is how I reach you through my rhymes
>
> sayin
> imagine if we bonded without the racist nonsense
> imagine everybody rich without all the hardships
>
> strugglin trying to bribe get the renters through their noggin
> imagine if Barack Obama didn't win and lost it
> we would be so divided from here to Austin
> but we still act like we aint got no conscience, (conscience)
> or we aint got no logic (logic)
>
> so where's the common sense we lost it
> damn

Cisco's "Imagine" Commercial (2012)

TEACHER: In the following video, think through these questions as you watch. (You might choose to list the questions on the board.)
- What does the video assume about the viewer?
- What images support the view of John Lennon's original text?
- What images do not, and why?
- What is the purpose of the video?

Watch the Cisco commercial: http://www.youtube.com/watch?v= qokjsUmuieA

Post-video discussion prompts:

- What does the video assume about the viewer? (Affordance of technology, happy families, etc.)
- Does it make a difference if you have never heard John Lennon's original version?
- What images support the view of Lennon's original text?
- What images do not, and why?
- What is the purpose of the video? (To persuade, to bring us joy, to celebrate differences, to "show" that a technology company can bring the world together.)
- Cisco is an American multinational corporation headquartered in San Jose, California, that designs, manufactures, and sells networking equipment. Whoever holds the rights to this song allowed Cisco to use the song this way.[5] What are the implications of this?

After the questions have been addressed, ask the class what image and ideal is being sold. Not technology but what ideal? What might Lennon feel about this interpretation, and why?

How you frame and set up dialogue matters. For instance, if you want students to get to the point that Cisco is using this music to sell something, then walk them through with guiding questions, rather than leading with that point. Many of us are struck by the beauty of the video and don't see any reason to question that Cisco is using this music to sell a product. If the conversation centers around whether Lennon would approve of this use, the conversation shifts from individual reactions to perspective.

Extension Activities

What would a collaborative piece or presentation look like as a final product?

- Create a photograph exhibit with the recording of "Imagine" playing in the background (or, better, a recording of the students performing/ singing).
- Improvise music over the chords of "Imagine" (C-major 7th and F-major 7th).
- Add movement to one of the versions.
- Create a Ti'Jean-like version (rap, hip-hop, spoken word).

Students will want to sing this. Too often, our experiences in these kinds of units are mediated by the recorded music and the video. Singing is the embodiment of their thinking and the conversations they had with others. Get them singing. P.S. 22, a public elementary school in New York City, has a chorus that performs this and many other popular music arrangements.[6,7]

"Everyday People" by Sly and the Family Stone (Grades 5–8 and Higher)

Sly and the Family Stone are one of the first interracial groups in the history of rock and roll. The band was made up of Sly Stone, his sister Rose, and their brother Freddie. Other members included Cynthia Robinson, a Black American singer and one of the first female trumpet players in an American rock-and-roll band; Greg Errico, drummer; Jerry Martini, saxophonist; and Larry Graham on bass. Responding to the "mixed personnel" of the band, sax player Jerry Martini recounted:

> It was deliberate. [Sly] told me about it before we even started the band. He was so hip on that. He was so far ahead of his time. He intentionally wanted a white drummer. There [were] a [ton] of black drummers that could kick Greg's ass and there was a lot of black saxophone players that could kick mine. He knew exactly what he was doing: boys, girls, black, white. (quoted in Lordi, 2012, p. 308)

When "Everyday People" was released in November 1968, the world had just experienced one of the most tumultuous years by any reckoning. Both Dr. Martin Luther King, Jr., and Senator Robert F. Kennedy were assassinated, and the Vietnam War had escalated to such a point that for the first time in history, families were daily and relentlessly exposed to TV images of death and destruction. Students were mobilizing and registering protest, and an increasing awareness of multiculturalism and the necessity of pluralism and living together presented "a new vision of participatory democracy" (Eyerman & Jamison, 1998, p. 109).

While the intersection of class and race within musicking (and in particular rock and roll) is beyond the scope of this chapter, it is important to recognize (and note in greater detail with students) that the emergence of what is thought of as rock and roll has been generally accepted to be part of wider patterns of "white appropriation of black musical traditions" (Eyerman & Jamison, 1998, p. 112). That said, during the 1960s, young people were changing the way audiences of mixed gender and races interacted with each other, and musical groups reflected this change. John Street (2012) makes a distinction between the ways in which musicians become political and what it means to be political. Stone did not align himself with any political movement per se, but he represented something very powerful that in essence was political. As an African-American man, rather than conveying anger and the antagonism that was reflected in (for instance) the Black Panther organization, Stone chose to model (through the group and his music) how one could live in the world with the other:

> [Sly Stone's] action in assembling a racially and gender-integrated unit spoke louder than any of his rare public declarations on racism, and the Family Stone, unlike some rock and folk acts, never manifested itself as part of the civil rights demonstrations or the movement overall. Instead, the band expressed its collective consciousness on the subject in musical form, most famously in "Everyday People." (Kaliss, 2008, p. 86)

At a time when people were demonstrating for peace, harmony, and goodwill among peoples, Sly and the Family Stone embodied what that actually meant. They worked together as a band (rather than a backup band with the focus primarily on a front person), and their previous recording, "Dance to the Music" (1967), was thought to be "a working model for how to reconcile the counterculture's conflicting desires of individual autonomy and communal togetherness" (Stone, 2006, p. 28). "Everyday People" extends that message as an exemplification of the way the band members wanted all of us to live in the world. It was how the Family Stone *were* living in the world.

The same lyrics of the song sung by a group that was not racially and gender-integrated would not have carried the same message, or it would have been a very different one, as we will see in the following lesson plans. "I am everyday people" meant exactly that. See me, see everyone, without judgment, without the ascription of value. Meet me for who I am—blue, green, rich, poor. "Different strokes for different folks" (Stone, 1968).

Sly and the Family Stone's "Everyday People" (1968)

In order to frame the rest of this unit, you need to locate the original recording of the song historically and politically. Do note with your students that there were many activist musicians, including John Lennon, and that the ways in which Sly and the Family Stone were engaging was one among many ways to challenge the times and subvert dominant power structures. If you are in a board or district that uses essential questions, there are many that would frame this unit as a larger interdisciplinary experience. Two possibilities might be:

- How and why do musics shift over time, and what makes this happen?
- Who and what stands to gain, and who and what stands to lose?

Listen to Sly and the Family Stone's "Everyday People." Make sure to listen to one of the original recordings, as the groove seems to get faster in future recordings. This is not a long song. Have them listen once and share with someone near them any reactions they have to the music. During the second listen, draw their attention to the lyrics (but do not yet pass out the lyrics). For the most part, in future iterations of the song in this chapter, the music itself does not change, only the presentation, purpose, and, eventually, text.

Have the following guiding questions up before playing the music a second time:

- How is the name of the group reflected in the lyrics of the song?
- What might be the purpose of this song?
- What meaning do you find in the lyrics?
- What line or lines sum up the song's message? (See Stone, 2006, p. 29.)

TEACHER: Work with a partner to talk these questions through. Write out your ideas; don't worry about writing in full sentences, but do get your thoughts down. Bring this back to the full class, and start a list of ideas for a flip chart. We will want to return to this when we listen to other versions and performances of this song.

Watch a video of "Everyday People." There are different video recordings of this. It is best if you can find one of the original performances as the first video you show to the students.

Post-video discussion prompts:

- Now that you have watched the video, what other thoughts do you have?
- Are you hearing the music differently? If so, in what ways?
- What did you notice about the performance?
- What is the purpose of this song? Has this changed for you?
- What is the mood of the performers? (Provide examples.)

It may not mean much to students in the 21st century, but a female trumpet player, and one who is a Black American, was and continues to be a big deal. Also, the racial mix of the group may not seem unusual to students now, but it was profound in 1968. Remind them that the Civil Rights Act was not signed into law until 1964, so theoretically (and for instance), if this band had begun any earlier than 1964 (they became an official group in 1967) and traveled together in the South previous to 1964, they all may not have been able to stay in the same hotels. You can mention the Marcels, an earlier multiracial doo-wop group, who did indeed suffer these indignities when traveling.

Pass out the lyrics to the song, and play the video again.

Now that the lyrics are in front of them, have them think through the following questions (found in Stone, 2006):

- How would you describe the way Sly Stone sings the line "We got to live together"?
- What is the significance of the line "There is a long hair that doesn't like the short hair"?
- In the discourse of the '60s, what did hair suggest about an individual's age, cultural preferences, and political leanings?
- Who would have long hair?
- Who would have short hair?
- Would the meaning change if Stone scolded short hairs for disliking long hairs?

Follow up by highlighting another variation on this theme: "There is a yellow one that won't accept the black one / That won't accept the red one that won't accept the white one" (Stone, 2006, p. 29).

Again, make sure to note responses somewhere (flip chart) so that you can return to them as you move through to other versions and covers of *Everyday People*.

Joan Jett and the Blackhearts' Version of "Everyday People" (1983)

I was angry at a world that gave girls shit for playing guitar. (Joan Jett, 2018)

Deborah Harry, Joan Jett, and Madonna are female icons who pushed the boundaries of power and sexuality. They were three completely different musicians, each creating in a different genre, and no discussion of rock and roll with students should ignore the contributions of these women. Each came of age during a time when the 1970s feminist movement was taking the world by storm; each was forced to weather insult and derision for the crime of being female performers in a world dominated by men.[8]

It is important to situate Jett before thinking through her video version of "Everyday People." As one of the original members of the all-female band the Runaways, early on she saw the potential of music as a force, indeed, music as "subversive noise" (Attali, 1985, p. 7). Her music situated her as a serious rock musician with serious guitar chops. Before playing this version of "Everyday People," you might want to share with your students a video of "Bad Reputation" (1981) so that they have a visual sense of Jett's playing and persona. The juxtaposition of "Bad Reputation" with her "Everyday People" video will help students think through the choices she decided to make with the visual representation of the song.

You will also need to attend to the time frame in which this video was recorded. The ethos of the '60s, drowned out by the cultural turmoil of the '70s, was long gone. In its place were Reaganomics and Thatcherism, economic conservatism that benefited those who were already privileged. Materialism and consumerism took hold of people's focus and attention, consequently defining individuality over the communal and hyper-individualism over pluralism. It is interesting to note that this was the beginning of the MTV era as well, so as of November 1981, music videos and the visuals embedded in them became part and parcel of what it meant to market not just one's creations but one's persona, or "brand" in contemporary terms.

Begin this segment by playing the recording—no visuals. Ask students to note the musical differences they are hearing. Then ask them to reflect back on the original Sly and the Family Stone version and compare the two.

- Knowing what we know about Joan Jett, why would she choose to perform this song?
- What meaning do you think she finds in the lyrics?
- What is she trying to convey to listeners when she sings these words?
- What do you think she means when she sings "We got to live together"? (Remind them of the discussion you had when you listened to Sly Stone's version. This would be the time to bring out the flip chart from the previous discussions.)

Next, play the video from the same year the song was released (1983) directed by David Mallet: https://www.dailymotion.com/video/x217op

If for some reason you can't access the video, students will get a sense of what is happening in the video from the following description:

> The video opens with the viewer seeing only Jett's feet in tennis shoes, jogging to the beat as the music begins. She is then seen buying a newspaper, where she opens the page to a cartoon titled "Joan Jett & the Blackhearts." These images are juxtaposed throughout the video with the band (dressed in black leather jackets, chains, etc.) playing "Everyday People" on a studio set decorated with gates and torches. After each time we see Jett out in the world, we return to the visuals of her singing the exact same version we heard previously. In essence, throughout the video, we see Jett going through her daily activities, except in each scenario, something goes wrong. She shuts off her alarm, and it falls apart. She looks in the mirror to check her hair, and the mirror falls off the wall. She opens up the refrigerator, and everything falls out. She attempts to dry her hair, and the blow dryer catches on fire. She is heating up milk, and it boils over at the same time as the toaster catches on fire. She goes out to eat (at a McDonald's), and the hamburger explodes ketchup on her white T-shirt. She tries to hail a taxi, and it drives past, splashing water all over her. She ends her frustrating day by jumping at last into bed, and the bed falls apart.

- What meaning is now being conveyed in the lyrics?
- What is Jett trying to express to listeners when she sings these words?
- What is she asking us to consider when she sings "We got to live together"?
- Has the purpose of the song changed with the addition of these visuals?
- Is Joan Jett everyday people?

Clearly, this interpretation is a far cry from the original intent of Sly and the Family Stone. The goal is to help students come to that conclusion and contemplate in what ways the music has been co-opted by the visuals to send a very different message. What complexities compelled Jett to make this video?

"Everyday People" as Found and Used in Commercials

This song and its pliable message lend itself to the machinery of production and consumption. The goal here is to refer back to the Cisco commercial that used "Imagine" in order to sell its products without really talking about the products and think through what is happening here with the use of "Everyday People." Chison Belcher (who seems to be about all things cars) has posted several commercials that use "Everyday People" on his YouTube channel.[9] He includes TV commercials that use both the music and the message to advertise products. The Toyota commercials, unlike the clear co-optation of "Imagine" in the Cisco commercial, vary in purpose and intent, with Toyota's "Everyday" campaign being the exception.

On one end of the spectrum, there is an interesting commercial from Australia with people from all walks of life using their Toyotas in different ways. This seems to fall under a larger campaign where actors focus on the word *everyday*, as in "I will strive to spend more time with my children—every day." On the other end of the spectrum, in the category of barely bothering with the music, falls one of the many US commercials advertising leasing and finance rates for local car dealerships in Michigan.

There is also a Smarties candy commercial that uses duets for each line of the song.[10] The singing and imagery are actually quite beautiful (until the animated Smarties fill the final screen). What is so fascinating about this example, however, is that there are at least two other videos of people covering the Smarties cover! In one of the covers, the singer actually introduces the version by saying, "I am going to sing 'Everyday People' *from the Smarties commercial*" (emphasis added), as if this *is* the song.[11] And indeed, she sings a version of the melody found only in the Smarties commercial. Sigh . . .

I would suggest that this assignment be something students could work on in small groups, tracking down versions and using the following kinds of guiding questions to think issues through.

- What are the aims of the commercial?
- Who is the target audience for the commercial?
- What emotions are being evoked as you watch? Might there be a different reaction for the intended target audience?

- What visuals are being used?
- What symbols or metaphors are being used to convey meaning?
- How is the music being used to make each of the above points?

Playing For Change and "Everyday People"

For a completely different usage of "Everyday People," have the students watch the Playing For Change video: https://www.youtube.com/watch?v=-g4UWvcZn5U. This is one of those videos that brings tears to the eyes of adults—particularly music teachers. Each vignette pairs a school in need and musicians in order to raise awareness of successes in schools.

Playing For Change is a movement created to inspire and connect the world through music, born from the shared belief that music has the power to break down boundaries and overcome distances between people. Our primary focus is to record and film musicians performing in their natural environments and combine their talents and cultural power in innovative videos we call Songs Around The World. Creating these videos motivated us to form the Playing For Change Band—a tangible, traveling representation of our mission, featuring musicians met along our journey; and establish the Playing For Change Foundation—a separate 501(c)3 nonprofit organization dedicated to building music and art schools for children around the world. Through these efforts, we aim to create hope and inspiration for the future of our planet. (Playing For Change, 2020)

Playing For Change was created as an activist platform. In this case, "Everyday People" is being used to raise money for music and arts schools. It would be fabulous at this point if students were to create a similar kind of video in the school, or even in the community, to raise awareness for a cause of their choice. Students desire to be activists; why not provide the platform for change?

Arrested Development's Version, "People Everyday" (1992)

I would be remiss in not including this version. In fact, the genesis for these plans came out of my love for it. I was aware of the Sly and the Family Stone original, but this music really spoke to me. Much like Ti'Jean's cover of "Imagine," Arrested

Development takes "Everyday People" and reframes the story to highlight an experience of one of the group members in and with the everyday. They use the melody when they sing "I am everyday people," but the text (story) changes, and much of the singing becomes spoken text. The song has an amazing groove, and the images both celebrate and reflect problematic aspects of day-to-day life. Note, however, that the musicians refer to themselves using the N-word. There is a performance at the Kennedy Center in which they themselves change the lyrics,[12] but I urge you to make the argument with your principal to use the original video[13] and incorporate dialogue that discusses the importance of how the word is being used referentially in the text, with a deliberate and intended function. Perhaps it's obvious but bears stating, that the intention here is not to normalize the N-word, but to further clarify that Black Americans historically have reclaimed this word that has served as an expression of white supremacy and hate. There is a powerful (clever and intelligent) video with Ta-Nehisi Coates[14] addressing the relationship communities have with words (in particular this one) that could be used as rationale. Play this video with your students before playing either of the Arrested Development versions. Even if you do use the version where the word is silenced, students will recognize its presence, particularly as you should pass out the lyrics for deeper comprehension, so this dialogue needs to be part of the encounter one way or the other.

Possible guiding questions (much like above):

- What are the aims of this version?
- Who is the intended audience for the version?
- What emotions are being evoked as you watch? Might there be a different reaction for different audiences?
- What visuals are being used, and why?
- What symbols or metaphors are being used to convey meaning?
- How is the music being used to make each of the above points?

Extension Activities

What would a collaborative piece or presentation of "Everyday People" look like as a final product?

Just as was suggested with "Imagine," "Everyday People" would be an easy piece of music to learn and perform. A reimaged visual interpretation of this song situating it in this decade would be interesting.

Lingering Issues

> There is all the difference in the world between having something to
> say and having to say something. (Dewey, 1907, p. 67)

At the time of writing this book, Sweden's Greta Thunberg (age 16) was sailing across the ocean to New York on a racing yacht equipped with solar panels in order to speak at the 2019 UN Climate Action Summit. Almost single-handedly, this young woman has brought worldwide attention to the climate crisis. Young people all over the world have risen to her challenge and have staged school walkouts and strikes for the climate. Blaming adults for the place in which we now find ourselves, Thunberg has been relentless in presenting the issues through a lens of responsibility and science.

Perhaps even more powerful, however, is the Black Lives Matter movement. All over the world people are calling for attention to systemic racism in our institutions, including schools. Students are demanding change, taking to the streets and social media, petitioning, protesting, and marching. They are organizing,

> [propagating] resources and information for others to become educated about
> the pressing need to strive for racial justice. Students share links to petitions, offer
> advice for safe protesting practices, create templates for emailing authorities, list
> bail funds and black-owned restaurants and businesses in need of support, and
> share videos documenting instances of police brutality at protests. (Rim, 2020,
> para 3)

As these are important and powerful social movements in our lives, musicians are of course responding in a variety of ways, whether by raising awareness or creating and even repurposing protest songs for these moments. Students are already involved to varying degrees in efforts of community-based activism, thus we honor and reflect these causes when we address these initiatives in our music classrooms. The goal is to both help students understand the complex issues of the politics of song and to provide spaces for students to creatively articulate their nuanced understandings of these issues.

Students want these kinds of conversations; they are having them with or without us and I believe they deserve these conversations with us to help facilitate. They long to have spaces where they can talk freely about issues that are meaningful to them; that help them name their world and their own challenges of navigating the everyday. It is interesting to ponder whether Dewey (1907) might consider popular music tunes, and the replication of those, as "ready-made materials" (p. 48). Music teachers must facilitate how students come to listen in the world and to the world, so that these musics, these moments, aren't simply something we passively absorb "[marking] dependency of one mind upon another" (p. 48). The two pieces of music presented in this chapter are two among many that frame the kinds of entry points that interrogate materials often made for and treated as "made for listening" (p. 48). I offer these two because of the ways in which they have been used over time and as a possible blueprint for bringing genuine dialogue into the music classroom.

7

Policy and Teaching

Establishing Change—In Conversation with Patrick Schmidt

In many ways, I have been hanging around the fringes of policy since I wrote my dissertation. Except I didn't know it. At the time, I thought I was "just" looking at documents and wondering how they came to be what they were. I remember sitting down so very long ago with Patrick Jones at a conference, asking him to teach me what policy was. He looked at me and said, "Your dissertation is a policy document." Two things bear noting. First, how wonderful to have someone in your life to whom you can turn and ask questions without the fear of humiliation. And second, how startled I was to realize how multifaceted the concept of policy was. I had no idea I could have any influence on anything connected to policy. I had been the quintessential elementary music teacher who closed her door and interacted with the principal (and even other teachers) only when I needed something for my program.

But this doesn't fully explain why I chose to include a chapter that addresses policy in a book that suggests we transcend day-to-day policies that seemingly inhibit the interactions I am asking us to take on. Consider this, though. If what I'm asking us to consider stays only in our classrooms, and we only *hope* that our engagements move beyond our classrooms and into the world, that hope is not enough. This is the hope of fatalism. And once we succumb to fatalism, as Freire (1994) writes, it "becomes impossible to muster the strength we absolutely need for a fierce struggle that will re-create the world" (p. 8). Freire reminds us that the hope we need is a critical hope anchored in activism. As Schmidt writes below, "policy know-how and framing capacity" is one activist way forward and, I conjecture, one that Freire might see as a way to "unveil opportunities for hope, no matter what the obstacles may be" (Freire, 1994, p. 9).

Music and Social Justice. Cathy Benedict, Oxford University Press (2021). © Oxford University Press.
DOI: 10.1093/oso/9780190062125.003.0008.

In Conversation with Patrick Schmidt

I present here my dialogue with Patrick Schmidt, a leading researcher in music education policy, because we need to have a better understanding of the power we do wield when it comes to making the changes I am asking us to make. Shutting our door only to open it when we need something undermines the kind of dialogue I have been describing throughout the book. Thus, I recognize a need to be more cognizant and aware of new ways of being that are grounded in tools and strategies that are well within our reach.

CATHY: So, welcome, Patrick. Help us think through how your research in policy supports the message embedded in this book.

PATRICK: First off, thanks for this opportunity. Working with teachers is, for me, where everything begins, which suggests that at the school level, policy should be considered a pedagogical practice. For many in the teaching profession, policies are seen as external, constraining, disabling; and many are. But this perception colors and hampers the potential for policy work by teachers within schools and communities. I believe that music educators concerned with social justice—which includes fighting for equitable labor conditions where teachers can be autonomous and critical—should look closer at policy and its practice as a constitutive part of their professional lives.

I believe in the pedagogical vision of this book. The kind of pedagogical engagements addressed here depend on critical awareness and thoughtful interaction. This is quite different from teaching that is prescribed, fully structured, and largely non-adaptive. I've suggested (Schmidt, 2019) that pedagogical action can be said to begin with and be situated by questions such as What matters, and why? I believe thoughtful teachers enter their classrooms every day asking the question, What matters to my students and to me, in this context, today? The decisions that follow, then, delineate one's practice—what is to be done and learned and how—which then lead to reflexive questions, such as Who benefited from my decisions? Who did not (or less so), and why? Just as significant, I would argue that these exact same questions and the dispositions behind them animate thoughtful policy.

CATHY: For those of us who may not have an understanding of how you are imagining policy and what impact we do have, how might you help us to understand better?

PATRICK: My work tries to highlight that policy takes many shapes and thus "can be formal or informal, obvious or subtle, soft or hard, implicit or explicit" (Schmidt,

2017, p. 2). When asked, people usually make no distinctions between *policies* or policy texts (those things enacted in forms of rules or legislations) and *policy* (meaning, a practice that is negotiated between individuals, in multiple contexts, daily). It's absolutely true that policies consist of things such as norms and regulations, made legitimate because of custom or historical precedent. But these policies come to exist *because of* policy practices, which consist of ideas, negotiated by people, and whose adoption and implementation can lead to profound outcomes.

In fact, to make this clearer, we might consider how the Supreme Court perfectly represents this point. In both Canada and the United States, nine justices, through artful dialogue and interaction, establish the most consequential policies of the land. What they do, their daily work—deliberating, assessing, listening, dialoguing, pedagogically questioning, and ultimately making decisions about what matters, to whom, and why—is what I have been calling policy practice. Their rulings, and the consequent cascade of texts they generate, are policies.

CATHY: But how do you respond to people who say, "I'm just one person. What can I possibly do?"

PATRICK: Critical teachers take agency and participation seriously. They value their own autonomy and work at it by developing their professional know-how and framing capacities. At the same time, they place their autonomy in relation to their own contexts, that is, to the needs, values, and challenges of the communities around them (Kincheloe, 2008). Critical and caring teachers deliberate, critique, and enact work *with* students. To me, that's at the center of critical pedagogies, as well as at the center of *policy practice*. While I don't have the space to address all that is involved here,[1] I do want to offer that there are three areas of action that every music teacher can consider as they think through policy practice and their role in it: *conscientization, participation,* and *activism*.

In some ways, the practices that you're asking for in this book are a manifestation of conscientization, which emerges out of a constant interplay between framing (what to do and why to do something), action, engagement (with the other), and reframing. And this is similar to the pedagogy of Paulo Freire, to whom you have referred throughout this book, as he used generative ideas to trigger known realities and experiences as a point of departure for pedagogical interaction. That's why I wanted to start with conscientization, to argue that, much as you did with hope, *voice*, defined as the access and capacity to express an opinion, while key, is insufficient. Voice has to move toward agency, acting and engaging with and for others, which in turn moves to conscientization, the capacity to frame issues as they require adaptation, to see with variant lenses, and, as important, to be compelled to act and thus to imagine alternative ways of acting.

[CATHY]: I am so happy you used the word *conscientization*. When I read Freire and ask others to read Freire, this word often feels so impenetrable, not to mention almost impossible to pronounce for first language English speakers. To me, this word and concept mean developing a deep understanding of our world, our relationships in it, its inherent contradictions, and how we may act on them. I also see this idea as directly connected to encouraging students to name their worlds as we afford the space for critical reflection in our curriculum and our pedagogical encounters. Here you are connecting this to our ability and need as teachers to name our contexts and as a way of moving toward recognizing how those contexts came to be and how we can participate in envisioning new possible engagements.

PATRICK: Indeed, at the center of policy practice is participation, for it signals the ways in which our collective obligations are "organized in specific locales and through specific groups of people who can decide what is reasonable for the processes of change" (Popkewitz, 2010, p. 421). We are the locus of action, a fact that is true for both pedagogy and policy practice. My point here is that the idea that teachers ought not to participate in policy processes seems to me just as absurd as teacher-proof curricula, where pedagogical engagement is reduced to a sequence of talking points.[2]

> Imagine that your school has a mission statement on inclusion that states "inclusion is not simply an end in itself, but a means to an end. It is about contributing to the realization of an inclusive society" (Liasidou, 2012, p. 87). This policy text sets the conditions. But in reality, it is the enactment of the text that will "make or break" how the policy is felt, meaning that the way the school community acts as it attempts to enact or live the policy will determine what inclusion *actually* means in that context, that is, how it is experienced, not in general terms but individually.

CATHY: Which logically leads to the notion of activism, which for me needs to be understood as a form of participation as leadership, again following Freire, who saw reflection and action as inseparable from each other.

PATRICK: Yes, and central to this point is what you have essentially been saying throughout the book. Developing *leadership*—another word for policy practice—means investing in *the ability to act with others*, to develop work that is self- and other-oriented. I find the work of Sachs (2003) informative here, as I believe this speaks to activism as part of policy practice and is essential to the kind of pedagogical aims explored in this book. For Sachs, activism involves:

inclusiveness rather than exclusiveness;
collective and collaborative action;
recognition of the expertise of all parties involved;
creating an environment of trust and mutual respect;
being responsive and responsible;
acting with passion;
experiencing pleasure and having fun. (pp. 147–149)

In my mind, what emanates from this is a relationship between a right to participate and a responsibility to act—which is what I would place at the center of activism.

CATHY: Throughout the book, I've tried to convey how challenging I know it is to
change one's practice. And while I have used polices to support the points
I am making, I've done so knowing this is a place where we can begin to enter
conversations with school boards, districts, principals, teachers, and even
parents. But I realize I am referencing these as if they are there only to be used as
justification.

PATRICK: You're not incorrect in referencing these documents as justification. Policies
abound related to complex issues and how they intersect within classrooms. For
example, we battle and struggle for policies that would create the conditions
for cultural diversity to be established as a universal value. We fight for policies that stave off extremism in all its forms. We uphold the ethical parameters
that incentivize integration, that honor Indigenous voices, expose racism, and
combat gender inequity. However, if these policies are not lived in *policy practice*
within our classrooms, our schools, our lives, their impact is lessened and their
expression muted.

The recent curricular reforms in the province of British Columbia (British
Columbia Ministry of Education, 2015) radically reposition Indigenous musics
as central to regional and national identity. They call for classroom materials
and resources to be developed in cooperation with local Indigenous community leaders and musicians. As the most progressive state-supported efforts in
Canada, British Columbia's initiatives provide hope and a model for action and
thought. Challenges emerge, however, when these ideals are brought into practice, and they are clearly represented in the questions you raise throughout this
book, as even best intentions can become token actions, implemented in this-is-
good-enough fashion, which allow business as usual to continue under the ve-
neer of change.

The evidence is in the pedagogical practice—in other words, how teachers and
students will engage and construct the issue with each other, what choices are
made, how musics are set up, what conversations are suppressed. The "problems"
of indigeneity in the music classroom—whose music, what rights I have toward

it, how music and social norms overlay, in what ways tradition and innovation intersect—are also the problems of indigeneity within schools: whose knowledge, what is the role of colonial institutions such as schools, and in what ways distinct ways of thinking and interacting can be used or appropriated in the new context. All these are representations of policy practice in action, that is to say, how general policy ideas come to be represented and made manifest in daily action.

CATHY: These are the questions we too often shy away from, believing (even sometimes hoping) others will take care of these for us. And these are exactly the kinds of questions I've been saying we should be modeling and opening up to our students. Serious and mindful engagement with these issues *is* the work of policy practice, and these engagements must be done by all of us, including administrators, community members, and, of course, teachers and students.

PATRICK: Exactly! And to pick up on the mandate to indigenize curriculum that we just discussed, we need to understand, for instance, how there is no such a thing as simply "implementing" an Indigenous-conscious curriculum. This requires relationship building, ongoing trial and risk-taking, resources, and pedagogical adaptation. In my terms, this is the sustained negotiation that I call policy practice. Policies are the easy bit. Policy practice, the processes we engage in every day in making decisions about what matters and how it will take shape in our work, is where the rubber meets the road.

CATHY: One reason I felt it necessary to include a chapter that addresses policy (although I now see that it's limiting to simply use the word *policy*, as it does little to render fully the points you've been making) is that throughout the book, I've tried to link my thinking and actions to ethical "oughts" and ethical imperatives. I've also tried to connect this thinking to the importance of reflexivity so that we might better understand ways we might be complicit in reproducing systems we do not want to reproduce.

PATRICK: Yes! It's the same thinking that guides my own understanding of these processes. I believe that ethical imperatives compel music educators to familiarize themselves with policy because "policy discourses work to privilege certain ideas and topics and speakers and exclude others" (Ball, 2009, p. 5). In other words, if we are not actively participating in the policy practice of our schools and boards and communities, others will fill that void. For decades, the field of music education has attempted to enter the realm of policy by betting on advocacy. In so doing, our field has often viewed policy as the authoritative allocation of values, expressed in words.[3] Today we need to acknowledge that this strategy has proven limited and that our engagements with policy must be expanded. The imperative for music education in the highly political 21st-century reality is a shift from advocacy to a direct focus on educational policy capacity. If we learned to demystify the notion of policy as a rarefied area of influence and something beyond our reach, we could come to see policy as requiring active and personal participation.

CATHY: I'm hearing you tell us that if we become convinced that advocacy done by others is insufficient (even when it's done by our own professional organizations), we will invest in developing our own policy practice. The connections between Buber's (1947/2002) pedagogy of "mutual relationship" and your vision for policy practice provide a new way of seeing our agency—not as something we have to become but as something we already can be. If we embrace Buber's thinking, policy can be seen as "a means of sense making, a way in and through which we represent, interrogate, and interpret experience and come to know ourselves and [each other]" (Barrett & Stauffer, 2012, p. 1). And I love that, of course!

Patrick, thank you so much for connecting the ideas in this book to policy practices. If there were one thing you would like to leave us with, what would that be?

PATRICK: I would invite music teachers to begin by asking themselves a simple question: *What does policy participation look like for me?* This small act, only mildly subversive, might elicit some powerful new beginnings. Beginnings are hard, and much of what you've been asking throughout this book might feel like a whole lot of beginnings. And perhaps bringing policy to the equation might just feel like one more thing to add to the plate. But as Julie Andrews would sing, "Nothing comes from nothing, nothing ever would,"[4] and thus begin we must.

Afterword

> The meaning of this dialogue is found in neither one nor the other
> of the partners, nor in both added together, but in their interchange.
> (Friedman, 1965, p. 6)

Throughout this book, I have placed the importance of dialogue at the center
of our socially just engagements with the other. This has been a particular
kind of dialogue, one that attempts to remove the need of the individual as the
locus of interaction. In the above quote, Friedman reminds us that meaning is
not found in the point one is trying to further or even in the point one might
accept from the other. Meaning, rather, is found in the ongoing engagements
that form dialogue itself. But what does that even mean? And what does it
have to do with social justice?

Just exactly what *is* social justice was the topic of *The Oxford Handbook of
Social Justice in Music Education* (Benedict et al., 2015), a book I helped to
edit with the keen eyes of three colleagues. In that book, we reached out to
music educator-scholars all over the world to grapple with a concept that we
were concerned was becoming another trendy buzz phrase, an empty slogan.
As I was editing that book, and even writing my own chapter, I realized that
nowhere were we addressing what social justice might mean and look like at
the elementary level. It was almost as if social justice was only an appropriate
topic for those older than 16, the younger ones being perhaps not "developmentally" ready for whatever being ready meant. Perhaps, unfortunately, we
have come to equate social justice at the elementary level with Black History
Month or Hispanic Heritage Month or even Thanksgiving, where (at least)
more and more teachers are addressing issues of colonization. But studying
the work of others or, worse, having the work of others deposited into us—
Freire's (1993) banking concept of education—presents meaning as a thing
made rather than as a "thing in the making" (Ellsworth, 2005, p. 1). How we
come to "know" something is mediated in our engagements with all others.

Vivian Gussin Paley (1986) spent her lifetime observing young children
for the sole purpose of becoming for them a better listener and responder. In
this process, she learned to encourage wonderings and embraced the ways in
which children "intuitively approached [problems]" (p. 123). I love reading

Music and Social Justice. Cathy Benedict, Oxford University Press (2021). © Oxford University Press.
DOI: 10.1093/oso/9780190062125.003.0009.

Paley. I am able to see in myself those places she observed as her own. Those moments when we rush in to "help" the student think or answer for them the questions we have asked; filling in the blanks for them, essentially dismissing the way in which they approach both problem solving and problem posing. We are so sure we are helping them, and yet in doing so, we silence their thinking, their voice. Paley saw this kind of "help" as evidence that she was "teaching"—convinced "the appearance of a correct answer" (p. 122) was proof. Sharing with all of us this place of vulnerability, Paley forges ahead, willing to reshape her pedagogical encounters:

> The question was not how would I enter but, rather, what were the effects of my intervention? When did my words lead the children to think and say more about their problems and possibilities, and when did my words circumvent the issue and silence the actors? When did my answers close the subject? (pp. 124–125)

I contend that *these* are the questions we should post as the "rules of the classroom." Socially just encounters depend on reflexive responses; students absolutely understand being silenced and as such are more than able to move beyond agreeing and disagreeing into spaces of critical, thoughtful, meaningful, genuine dialogue.

I experience daily how important it is to establish a classroom where "confusion—mine or theirs—is as natural a condition as clarity" (Paley, 1986, p. 131). I am not sure I understood how important it was to share this until I read Paley's words again. There are generations of students in my wake who are more than likely to think back to our pedagogical encounters as confusing, meandering; clearly, I am not a point-A-to-point-B thinker. To this day, I often cannot shake the feeling that my kind of thinking rarely counts for much in contexts outside of classrooms. However, in classrooms, I have learned to establish an environment where students come to understand that clarity (as they have come to know it) means little to me in terms of them "earning a good grade." This takes time, as they have all been "trained" into a system where grades and marks have everything to do with comparisons and very little to do with learning. However, I persevere, for reasons ethical, social, and musical. Thus, we consider throughout our (too often) short time together that clarity and surety rarely lead to humility, rarely lead toward care, and almost always leave them without space for forgiveness—in particular, a space for them to be forgiving toward themselves.

The music education university students with whom I interact have a limited and limiting sense of musicianship. Theirs is a conception grounded in the kind of listening I have challenged throughout this book: "ready-made one-way [musicianship] and inert listening" (Waks, 2011, p. 202). This breaks my heart, as clarity for them is me telling them how it should be done, me giving the grade based on the fact that they have done what I told them to do. I shall never forget midway through a yearlong class where we had been discussing participation and growth *daily*, when Naomi composed the most gloriously interesting and beautiful Mixolydian canon. She taught it, and we sang it in canon as a class. As each canon part entered, we could feel the other connecting to this music, we could feel ourselves realizing the beauty, we could hear one another rise to the musical encounter, bringing this composition alive as a true I-thou encounter. There was silence after we finished. Then great joy and applause. I moved to Naomi and reached out to her. Not knowing what to say, I remarked that this response from all of us surely was better than me giving her an A. In the seconds it took for her to respond, I realized she actually had to consider that question. And this is the great tragedy of sacrificing our personal engagements with one another and with beauty for the pursuit of ready-made clarity. I had assumed she would recognize the power of this moment. Sadly, she did not. Not at first, anyway.

Nothing ever happens at first. Well, things, of course, happen at first, but as Hannah Arendt (1958) reminds us: "It is in the nature of beginning that something new is started which cannot be expected from whatever may have happened before" (pp. 177–178). I believe in the something new started—a rethinking, a reimagining, a re-engagement with what we thought we knew to be true. Socially just engagements are these new beginnings, pedagogical encounters in which we listen and attend in ways that vow humility, recognition, and agency. I am forever in debt to students who have insisted that I think differently and be different. I am forever in debt to my colleagues and the authors I have read who reminded me that beginning again and again with confusion and wonderment is not simply a socially just action but the only action available to us if we desire a world made in common, thoughtfully and meaningfully, with care for one another.

Notes

Chapter 2

1. I am not assuming everyone "knows" this song. In fact, we should never assume something is ever "common" knowledge. This song can be found very easily on the internet and in many song book collections. The idea is to begin with the version that uses the language "buy" as in "Papa's gonna buy you a mockingbird").
2. For an accessible interview with Ma and his thinking about collaborations, listen to or read "Yo-Yo Ma on Successful Creative Collaboration," https://hbr.org/ideacast/2016/05/yo-yo-ma-on-successful-creative-collaboration.html

Chapter 3

1. At the final writing of this manuscript, the world was engulfed in the COVID-19 pandemic. Social-media platforms as well as national news agencies were filled with people making music as a way to make sense of the pandemic and as a way to celebrate our lived humanity.
2. Universal Design for Learning emerged out of architectural design for buildings and products. Originally focused on changing spaces to accommodate all peoples (closed captioning in media doesn't just help those with hearing issues; imagine being in a loud space and unable to hear important weather announcements, for instance). The same principles have been embraced in education. One example in the elementary classroom would be to demonstrate how to play games in multiples ways: you can use your finger to motion turning rather than walking in a circle. The goal is that no one feels singled out, and everyone benefits from the multiple means of representation, action, and expression and of engagement.
3. These are just guiding questions. You can certainly also help the students think about friendship in more depth. What kind of friendship does Tubby have with the Frog? How did that friendship come to be?
4. Whether to capitalize the B in Black American is contested terrain. On June 26, 2020 the New York Times addressed this very issue in their article published days before the proofs of these chapters were returned to the publisher: "A Debate Over Identity and Race Asks, Are African-Americans 'Black' or 'black'?" As of now the Associated Press, which often sets the tone for journalism, has chosen capital B, while the New York Times and the Washington Post are still deliberating. Outside of journalism, Brittney Cooper (for instance) calls our attention to the historical context of enslavement, identity, and continued struggle, "In the choice to capitalize, we are paying homage to a history with a very particular kind of political engagement" (para 4). However, others believe that using the capital B turns the word into a noun serving to "[lump] people of the African diaspora into a monolithic group and erases the diversity of their experiences" (para 7). I encourage everyone

to grapple with these issues as well as to read this article and others as they think through them. At this moment in time I choose a capital B. This book is geared toward grappling with larger systemic issues that are always in flux, constantly being re-examined through the lens of justice and equity, which we know often demands assertive action.

5. For an interesting read on the minstrel show, or minstrelsy, and the involvement of the composer of "O Canada" (Calixa Lavallée) in this movement, see Harris (2018).

6. When I received these chapters as proofs for my perusal, the Black Lives Matter movement was gaining significant momentum in forcing many to reexamine beliefs and actions, privilege, and complicity in contributing to systemic racist oppression. Decolonizing music education is no longer something one has heard about whispered faintly. Systemic racism pervades our repertoire, our pedagogy, our assumptions about others. Music organizations all over the world have posted statements on their websites promising transformation and action. While statements on websites can be valuable they must not remain as slogans, and what action looks like has to be mindfully thought through with those who have suffered bias and racism in ways that avoid burdening them with the responsibility of that labor. At the heart of this book is the belief that if genuine dialogue with the other begins early, we take these dispositions of critical and interrogative thinking forward with us as ways of being in the world.

7. "The Caldecott Medal was named in honor of nineteenth-century English illustrator Randolph Caldecott. It is awarded annually by the Association for Library Service to Children, a division of the American Library Association, to the artist of the most distinguished American picture book for children." http://www.ala.org/alsc/awardsgrants/bookmedia/caldecottmedal/caldecottmedal

8. The accompanying CD includes the sounds of a jazz ensemble bringing the words and images of the story to fuller life.

9. Don't skip this question. As Kelly Bylica makes clear in chapter 4, the sounds of a neighborhood are often an indicator of systematic disenfranchisement and/or privilege. Help the students think this through.

10. Citations for these books can be found in the references.

11. Children's Books Ireland. https://childrensbooksireland.ie/review/petars-song/

12. For more, see Oliveros (2005)https://soundartarchive.net/articles/Oliveros-1996-four_meditations_score.pdf

13. For more information on their publications addressing the compositional process with students, see Kaschub & Smith (2009, 2017).

14. If you do a quick web search, and I used Google, over 7,170,000 lesson plans were posted.

15. Some of those questions come from the Teaching Tolerance, Handout II: Anti-Bullying Reflection Questions, https://www.tolerance.org/sites/default/files/documents/bully_upper_handout2.pdf.

Chapter 4

1. See Cumberland (2001) for these and additional entry points and prompts.

2. The ideas Kelly is presenting here are only a very small reflection of her dissertation. For greater detail addressing the implementation of this project in two different US middle schools, see Bylica (2020).

Chapter 5

1. Elizabeth Gould (2007) urges music educators to consider that consensus may not be the "unproblematic virtue" we think it to be. She suggests, rather, that we must find "ways of maintaining relationship in the context of dissensus" (p. 237). Dissensus here aligns with the ways in which I have suggested that grappling with issues through continual dialogue is our continual way forward.

2. "Congress shall make no law respecting an establishment of religion, or prohibiting the free exercise thereof; or abridging the freedom of speech, or of the press; or the right of the people peaceably to assemble, and to petition the Government for a redress of grievances" (US Constitution, First Amendment).

3. While you are at it have the students problematize the word tribe and the usage of tribes. Many are addressing this (including the world of business), however, the Teaching Tolerance website has addressed this in the context of Black Americans: https://www.tolerance.org/magazine/spring-2001/the-trouble-with-tribe

4. The Arts curriculum in British Columbia has published *Indigenous Knowledge and Perspectives in K–12 Curriculum: Arts K–12*. https://curriculum.gov.bc.ca/curriculum/indigenous-education-resources/indigenous-knowledge-and-perspectives-k-12-curriculum

   The University of Toronto's Ontario Institute for Studies in Education, has a database dedicated to aboriginal peoples' curricula issues: "Deepening Knowledge: Resources for and About Aboriginal Culture." https://www.oise.utoronto.ca/deepeningknowledge/Teacher_Resources/Curriculum_Resources_(by_subjects)/Music/index.html

   The National Arts Centre: Arts Alive Canada has published *Celebrating Canada's Indigenous Peoples Through Song and Dance, Content and Music* by Sherryl Sewepagaham and Olivia Tailfeathers, which includes music written specifically for school contexts. http://artsalive.ca/pdf/mus/map/Indigenous-Teacher_Guide_en.pdf

5. This YouTube channel has almost two hours' worth of examples: https://www.youtube.com/watch?v=aCpcCZQOMtk

6. http://www.assnat.qc.ca/en/travaux-parlementaires/projets-loi/projet-loi-21-42-1.html?appelant=MC

7. Here, of course, is the issue to tease apart with students: one doesn't have to remove jewelry; it can be hidden under clothing.

8. Note that UNESCO has placed the Istanbul Hodjapasha Culture Center on its List of Intangible Cultural Heritage in order to both honor and protect the performances of the Mevlevi. This raises the point that these devotional songs can also be performed in public (and increasingly by women), which could deflect concerns surrounding religious practices (https://www.hodjapasha.com/en). Also note that Susan Steinman has written a thoughtful lesson plan that describes the context and originating practices: http://turkishculturalfoundation.org/education/files/37_Rumi_LESSON_PLAN_OUTLINE.pdf

9. For further reading, see A. Weisel, "Ravi Shankar on His Pal George Harrison and 'Chants of India,'" *Rolling Stone*. https://www.rollingstone.com/music/music-news/ravi-shankar-on-his-pal-george-harrison-and-chants-of-india-73258/

10. Their YouTube channel: https://www.youtube.com/channel/UCi9yJC0uqf4NXUkBNWl3kqw

11. For lesson plans and an in-depth look at the cultural context of Grenada, see Sirek (2019).

Chapter 6

1. https://education.kennedy-center.org/education/ceta/
2. For more information, see https://www.tc.columbia.edu/articles/2012/october/teachers-college-collaborates-on-study-guide-for-youngarts-m/. The program, however, has been discontinued.
3. A note about the links throughout this chapter. At the time of publishing the links were stable, but things change and you may have to search for new links.
4. You will need to situate *Glee*. As time goes by fewer students (and teachers) will know the show.
5. Yoko Ono entered into a new contract for global branding and rights management with Epic Rights in 2014. "Regardless of how we have experienced John Lennon—through his music, his art, his writings—he was defined by the message of love and peace, becoming an icon for generations worldwide," said Ono in a statement. "I regard the John Lennon Classic and Bag One Arts licensing programs as another way to honor John's legacy, and I am confident that by working closely with [Epic Rights CEO] Dell [Furano] and [his] team, we will achieve this goal." According to the press release, Ono would have personal approval of all licensed Lennon products. "We are committed to developing a worldwide licensing program that respects Lennon's beliefs and contributions to humanity, and anticipate strong global consumer demand from existing and new fans who want to connect with John Lennon and his legacy," said Furano in a statement." Spin, June 18, 2014. http://www.spin.com/2014/06/john-lennon-yoko-ono-licensing-brand-name-rights/
6. https://www.youtube.com/watch?v=lJNWs52d-08
7. For a discussion of fair use of copyright material—in this case, "Imagine": https://fairuse.stanford.edu/overview/fair-use/what-is-fair-use/
8. Note that as recently as 2016, Madonna was derided by Piers Morgan: "Oh she makes my skin crawl . . . you can't be 58 and prancing about like that." https://www.theguardian.com/music/musicblog/2016/dec/12/madonna-billboard-speech-women-pop-artists
9. Chison Belcher appears to be not only be a car aficionado but also an appreciator of "Everyday People." https://www.youtube.com/watch?v=8XsgOh6wUiM&list=PL2vK8PnXgiPgD0ABaTMRxothU-1jtx9BD
10. https://www.youtube.com/watch?v=lSkP5QbzZW4. For the Québécois in the room there are versions in French as well: https://www.youtube.com/watch?v=ATyXhvN8IcQ
11. https://www.youtube.com/watch?v=plQ7R8-Fi-o
12. https://www.youtube.com/watch?v=ohx0m2fR4zs
13. https://www.youtube.com/watch?v=JpRpNJF9T-M
14. https://www.youtube.com/watch?v=QO15S3WC9pg

Chapter 7

1. For details, see Schmidt (2019, chapter 3).
2. For those interested in knowing more, the work of Ball et al. (2012) offers one example of how teachers can work powerfully as policy actors in school change. Policy participation

is at the center of the work of Eric Shieh, a music teacher in New York public schools, documenting in practice how teacher-leaders can change school culture and pedagogical practice (Shieh, 2018).

3. For more on this, see the work of Ronald Heck (2004).

4. "Something Good," from *The Sound of Music* (1965).

References

Allsup, R. E. (2011). Popular music and classical musicians: Strategies and perspectives. *Music Educators Journal, 97*(3), 30–34. https://doi.org/10.1177/0027432110391810

American Council on Education. (1953). *The function of the public schools in dealing with religion*. Washington, DC: Committee on Religion and Education of the American Council on Education.

Andersen, K. (2018, March). How to talk like Trump: A short guide to speaking the president's dialect. *Atlantic*. https://www.theatlantic.com/magazine/archive/2018/03/how-to-talk-trump/550934/

Arendt, H. (1958). *The human condition*. Chicago: University of Chicago Press.

Asmar, M. (2019, December 3). Denver to change curriculum that educators said "eliminates the Native American perspective" *Chalkbeat*. https://chalkbeat.org/posts/co/2019/12/03/denver-to-change-curriculum-that-educators-said-eliminates-the-native-american-perspective/

Attali, J. (1985). *Noise: The political economy of music*. Minneapolis: University of Minnesota Press.

Aylesworth, J., & Gammell, S. (1995). *Old black fly*. New York: Henry Holt.

Ball, S. J. (2009). *The education debate*. Bristol: Policy.

Ball, S., Maguire, M., & Braun, A. (2012). *How schools do policy: Policy enactments in secondary schools*. London: Routledge.

Barrett, M. S., & Stauffer, S. L. (2012). Resonant work: Toward an ethic of narrative research. In M. Barrett & S. Stauffer (Eds.), *Narrative soundings: An anthology of narrative inquiry in music education* (pp. 1–17). Dordrecht: Springer Netherlands. https://doi.org/10.1007/978-94-007-0699-6

Benedict, C. (2006). Defining ourselves as other: Envisioning transformative possibilities. In C. Frierson-Campbell (Ed.), *Teaching music in the urban classroom* (Vol. 1) (pp. 3–13). Lanham, MD: Rowman & Littlefield.

Benedict, C., & O'Leary, J. (2019). Reconceptualizing "music making": Music technology and freedom in the age of neoliberalism. *Action, Criticism and Theory for Music Education, 8*(1), 26–43. https://doi.org/10.22176/act18.1.26

Benedict, C., Schmidt, P., Spruce, G., & Woodford, P. (Eds.). (2015). *The Oxford handbook of social justice in music education*. New York: Oxford University Press.

Berger, J. (2007). *Hold everything dear: Dispatches on survival and resistance*. New York: Pantheon.

Bezemer, J., & Kress, G. (2008). Writing in multimodal texts: A social semiotic account of designs for learning. *Written Communication, 25*(2), 166–195. https://doi.org/10.1177/0741088307313177

Biesta, G. (2010). *Good education in an age of measurement: Ethics, politics, democracy*. Herndon, VA: Paradigm.

Biesta, G. (2018). What if? Art education beyond expression and creativity. In G. Biesta, D. R. Cole, & C. Naughton (Eds.), *Art, artists and pedagogy: Philosophy and the arts in education* (pp. 11–20). New York: Routledge.

Bookman, A., & Morgen, S. (1988). *Women and the politics of empowerment*. Philadelphia: Temple University Press.

Bouma, G. (2017). Religions—lived and packaged—viewed through an intercultural dialogue prism. In F. Mansouri (Ed.), *Interculturalism at the crossroads: Comparative perspectives on concepts, policies and practices* (pp. 129–146). Paris: UNESCO.

British Columbia Ministry of Education. (2015). Building student success: BC's new curriculum. https://curriculum.gov.bc.ca/curriculum

Britzman, D. (1991). *Practice makes practice: A critical study of learning to teach.* Albany: State University of New York Press.

Brookfield, S., & Preskill, S. (1999). *Discussion as a way of teaching: Tools and techniques for democratic classrooms.* San Francisco: Jossey-Bass.

Brown, W. (2012). Civilizational delusions: Secularism, tolerance, equality. *Theory & Event, 15*(2). https://muse.jhu.edu/article/478356

Bruner, J. (2002). *Making stories: Law, literature, life.* Cambridge, MA: Harvard University Press.

Buber, M. (1947/2002). *Between man and man.* New York: Routledge.

Bylica, K. (2020). *Critical Border Crossing: Exploring Positionalities Through Soundscape Composition and Critical Reflection. Electronic Thesis and Dissertation Repository.* 7000. https://ir.lib.uwo.ca/etd/7000

Carle, E. (1996). *I see a song.* New York: Scholastic.

Children's Books Ireland. https://childrensbooksireland.ie/review/petars-song/

Crow, K., & Lester, M. (2008). *Cool daddy rat.* New York: Putnam Juvenile.

Cumberland, M. (2001). Bringing soundscapes into the everyday classroom. *Soundscape, 2*(2), 16–20.

Cusick, S. (2006). Music as torture/music as weapon. *Transcultural Music Review, 10.* http://www.sibetrans.com/trans/articulo/152/music-as-torture-music-as-weapon

Daniel, M., & Auriac, E. (2011). Philosophy, critical thinking and philosophy for children. *Educational Philosophy and Theory, 43*(5), 415–435. https://doi.org/10.1111/j.1469-5812.2008.00483.x

Delgado, R. (2013). Storytelling for oppositionists and others: A plea for narrative. In R. Delgado & J. Stefancic (Eds.), *Critical race theory: The cutting edge* (3rd ed.) (pp. 2411–2441). Philadelphia: Temple University Press.

Dewberry, D., & Millen, J. (2014). Music as rhetoric: Popular music in presidential campaigns. *Atlantic Journal of Communication, 22*(2), 81–92. https://doi.org/10.1080/15456870.2014.890101

Dewey, J. (1907). *The school and society.* Chicago: University of Chicago Press.

Dewey, J. (1964). *Democracy and education : An introduction to the philosophy of education.* New York: Macmillan.

Diamond, B. (2008). *Native American music in eastern North America: Experiencing music, expressing culture.* New York: Oxford University Press.

Dillon, D., & Dillon, L. (2002). *Rap a tap tap: Here's Bojangles—Think of that!* New York: Blue Sky.

Doharty, N. (2019). 'I felt dead': Applying a racial microaggressions framework to black students' experiences of Black History Month and black history. *Race Ethnicity and Education, 22*(1), 110–129. https://doi.org/10.1080/13613324.2017.1417253

Eisner, E., & Bird, L. (1998). *The kind of schools we need: Personal essays.* Portsmouth, NH: Heinemann.

Ellsworth, E. (2005). Places of learning: Media, architecture, pedagogy. New York: RoutledgeFalmer.

Evans, S. W. (2012). *We march.* New York: Roaring Brook.

Eyerman, R., & Jamison, A. (1998). *Music and social movements: Mobilizing traditions in the twentieth century.* Cambridge: Cambridge University Press.

Fecho, B., Coombs, D., & McAuley, S. (2012). Reclaiming literacy classrooms through critical dialogue. *Journal of Adolescent & Adult Literacy, 55*(6), 476–482. https://doi.org/10.1002/JAAL.00057

Fook, J. (1999). Reflexivity as method. *Annual Review of Health Social Science, 9*(1), 11–20. https://doi.org/10.5172/hesr.1999.9.1.11

Forst, R. (2013). *Toleration in conflict: Past and present.* Cambridge: Cambridge University Press.

Frazee, M. (2007). *Hush, little baby: A folk song with pictures.* Houghton Mifflin Harcourt.

Freedom Forum Institute. (2009). *Living with our deepest differences: Religious liberty in a pluralistic society.* https://www.religiousfreedomcenter.org/resources/textbooks-lessons/

Freire, P. (1970). *Pedagogy of the oppressed* (M. B. Ramos, Trans.). New York: Seabury. (Original work published 1968)

Freire, P. (1993). *Pedagogy of the oppressed* (rev. ed.). New York: Continuum International.

Freire, P. (1994). *Pedagogy of hope.* New York: Continuum International.

Freire, P. (2000). *Pedagogy of the oppressed* (30th anniv. ed.). New York: Continuum.

Friedman, C. (2005). *Nicky the jazz cat.* Brooklyn: PowerHouse.

Friedman, M. (1965). Martin Buber's final legacy: "The knowledge of man." *Journal for the Scientific Study of Religion, 5*(1), 4–9. https://doi.org/10.2307/1384249

Giles, C. (1994, January 10). Press-shy monks top the pop charts with greatest Gregorian chants. AP News. https://apnews.com/a0630a3ced61519cf8ae8a815019ab59

Giroux, H. (2017). Authoritarianism, class warfare, and the advance of neoliberal austerity policies. *Knowledge Cultures, 5*(1), 13–20. https://doi.org/10.22381/KC5120172

Giroux, H. (2018, August 2). Neoliberal fascism and the echoes of history. *Truthdig.* https://www.truthdig.com/articles/neoliberal-fascism-and-the-echoes-of-history/

Gollub, M., & Hanke, K. (2000). *The jazz fly.* Santa Rosa, CA: Tortuga.

Gorlinski, V. (2019). *Nueva canción.* Encyclopædia Britannica. https://www.britannica.com/art/nueva-cancion

Gould, E. (2007). Social justice in music education: The problematic of democracy. *Music Education Research: Music Education, Equity and Social Justice, 9*(2), 229–240. https://doi.org/10.1080/14613800701384359

Greene, M. (1995). *Releasing the imagination: Essays on education, the arts, and social change.* San Francisco: Jossey-Bass.

Greene, M. (2007). Imagination, oppression and culture: Creating authentic openings. https://maxinegreene.org/uploads/library/imagination_oc.pdf

Gutstein, E. (2006). *Rethinking mathematics: Teaching social justice by the numbers.* New York: Routledge.

Hall, L., & Piazza, S. (2010). Engaging with critical literacy: Reflections on teaching and learning. *English Journal, 99,* 91–94.

Hall, T., Lashua, B., & Coffey, A. (2008). Sound and the everyday in qualitative research. *Qualitative Inquiry, 14*(6), 1019–1040.

Hansen, D. T. (1993). The moral importance of the teacher's style. *Journal of Curriculum Studies, 25*(5), 397–421.

Hansen, D. T. (1994). Teaching and the sense of vocation. *Educational Theory, 44*(3), 259–275.

Hansen, D. T. (2005). Creativity in teaching and building a meaningful life as a teacher. *Journal of Aesthetic Education, 39*(2), 57–68.

Hansen, P. (2004). Hannah Arendt and bearing with strangers. *Contemporary Political Theory, 3*(1), 3–22. https://doi.org/10.1057/palgrave.cpt.9300124

Harris, R. (2018). *Song of a nation: The untold story of Canada's national anthem.* Toronto: McClelland & Stewart.

Heck, R. (2004). *Studying educational and social policy: Theoretical concepts and research method.* New York: Routledge.

Henkes, K. (1991). *Chrysanthemum.* New York: Greenwillow.

Hess, J. (2018). Challenging the empire in empir(e)ical research: The question of speaking in music education. *Music Education Research, 20*(5), 573–590. https://doi.org/10.1080/14613808.2018.1433152

Hess, J. (2019). Singing our own song: Navigating identity politics through activism in music. *Research Studies in Music Education, 41*(1), 61–80. https://doi.org/10.1177/1321103X18773094

hooks, b. (2000). *Feminist theory: From margin to center.* Cambridge, MA: South End.

Huber, P. L., & Solorzano, D. (2015). Racial microaggressions as a tool for critical race research. *Race Ethnicity and Education, 18*(3), 297–320. https://doi.org/10.1080/13613324.2014.994173

Hughes, L., & Collier, B. (2012). *I, too, am America.* New York: Simon & Schuster.

Irvine, J. J. (1991). *Black students and school failure: Policies, practices, and prescriptions.* Westport, CT: Praeger.

Isadora, R. (1979). *Ben's trumpet.* New York: Greenwillow.

Jeong, S., & Lee, B. H. (2013). A multilevel examination of peer victimization and bullying preventions in schools. *Journal of Criminology, 2013,* 10. https://doi.org/10.1155/2013/735397.

Jett, J. (2018). In P. Afterman & C. Brinkman (Producers) & K. Kerslake (Director). *Bad reputation.* https://www.youtube.com/watch?v=phbz4zD6Nso

Johnson-Eilola, J., & Wysocki, A. (2015). Interdisciplinarity after writing. *College Composition and Communication, 66*(4), 712.

Johnston, T., & Mazellan, R. (2004). *The harmonica.* Watertown, MA: Charlesbridge.

Kaliss, J. (2008). *I want to take you higher: The life and times of Sly and the Family Stone.* New York: Backbeat.

Kaschub, M., & Smith, J. (2009). *Minds on music: Composition for creative and critical thinking.* Lanham, MD: Rowman & Littlefield.

Kaschub, M., & Smith, J. (2017). *Experiencing music composition in grades 3–5.* New York: Oxford University Press.

Kelly, C. (2006). At peace with the wolf? Prokofiev's "official" Soviet works for children. *Three Oranges Journal, 12,* 3–9.

Kincheloe, J. L. (2008). *Knowledge and critical pedagogy: An introduction.* Dordrecht: Springer Netherlands.

Kirk, D. (1999). *Hush, little alien.* New York: Little, Brown Books for Young Readers.

Knaus, C. (2009). Shut up and listen: Applied critical race theory in the classroom. *Race Ethnicity and Education: Critical Race Praxis, 12*(2), 133–154. https://doi.org/10.1080/13613320902995426

Kramer, K., & Gawlick, M. (2003). *Martin Buber's I and Thou: Practicing living dialogue.* New York: Paulist.

Lalvani, P. (2015). "We are not aliens": Exploring the meaning of disability and the nature of belongingness in a fourth grade classroom. *Disability Studies Quarterly, 35*(4), p. 1–22.

Lee, C. (2011). What do we mean by literacy? Implications for literacy education. *Journal of Educational Thought, 45*(3), 255–266.

Liasidou, A. (2012). *Inclusive education, politics and policymaking.* New York: Continuum.

Long, S. (1997). *Hush little baby.* San Francisco: Chronicle.

Lordi, E. (2012). Fading out: White flight and Sly and the Family Stone's "Stand!" *Journal of Popular Music Studies, 24*(3), 305–315. https://doi.org/10.1111/j.1533-1598.2012.01337.x

Martin, D., Hanson, S., & Fontaine, D. (2007). What counts as activism? The role of individuals in creating change. *Women's Studies Quarterly, 35*(3–4), 78–94.

Mazzei, L. (2004). Silent listenings: Deconstructive practices in discourse-based research. *American Educational Research Association, 33*(2), 21–30.

Mitchell, P., & Binch, C. (2003). *Petar's song.* London: Frances Lincoln.

Musical development through listening. (1945). *Music Educators Journal, 31*(6), 46. https://doi.org/10.2307/3386630

National Association for Music Education. (1996). Sacred music in schools (position statement). https://nafme.org/my-classroom/music-selection/sacred-music/sacred-music-in-schools-position-statement/

National Coalition for Core Arts Standards. (2014). National Core Arts Standards: Dance, grades pre-K to 12. https://www.nationalartsstandards.org/sites/default/files/Dance%20at%20a%20Glance%20-%20new%20copyright%20info.pdf

National Council of Teachers of English. (2020a). About us. https://ncte.org/about/

National Council of Teachers of English. (2020b). Calls for manuscripts. https://secure.ncte.org/library/NCTEFiles/Resources/Journals/LA/0953-mar2018/LA0954Calls.pdf

Neumann, C. (2006). Chanting. In D. A. Stout (Ed.), *Encyclopedia of religion, communication, and media* (pp. 68–71). New York: Routledge.

Noddings, N. (1993). *Educating for intelligent belief or unbelief.* New York: Teachers College Press.

Noddings, N. (2003). *Caring: A feminine approach to ethics and moral education.* Los Angeles: University of California Press.

Noddings, N. (2008). The new outspoken atheism and education. *Harvard Educational Review, 78*(2), 369–390. https://doi.org/10.17763/haer.78.2.1777607445011272

Ocádiz Velázquez, G. (2020). *Music education in a liquid social world: The nuances of teaching with students of immigrant and refugee backgrounds* (Publication No. 6824) [Doctoral dissertation, University of Western Ontario]. Western University Electronic Thesis and Dissertation Repository.

Oliveros, P. (2005). *Deep listening: A composer's sound practice.* Lincoln, NE: iUniverse.

Ontario Arts Curriculum. (2009). Ministry of Education. http://www.edu.gov.on.ca/eng/curriculum/elementary/arts18b09curr.pdf

Ontario Language Arts. (2006). Ministry of Education. http://www.edu.gov.on.ca/eng/curriculum/elementary/language18currb.pdf

Ontario Social Studies Curriculum. (2018). Ministry of Education. http://www.edu.gov.on.ca/eng/curriculum/elementary/sshg18curr2013.pdf

Ornstein, M., & Kopelke, L. (2009). *The daddy longlegs blues.* New York: Sterling.

Paley, V. G. (1986). On listening to what the children say. *Harvard Educational Review, 56*(2), 122; 131–132. https://doi.org/10.17763/haer.56.2.p775487x30tk69m8

Petruish, A. (April 27, 2020). Brittany Howard's Transformation. *The New Yorker.* Retrieved from https://www.newyorker.com/magazine/2020/04/27/brittanyhowards-transformation.

Perrine, W. M. (2013). Religious music and free speech: Philosophical issues in *Nurre v. Whitehead. Philosophy of Music Education Review, 21*(2), 178–196. https://doi.org/10.2979/philmusieducrevi.21.2.178

Perrine, W. M. (2015). *Sacred music in public school curriculum: A philosophical inquiry into selected case law* (Publication No. 3702565) [Doctoral dissertation, Indiana University]. ProQuest Dissertations Publishing.

Perrine, W. M. (2016). The rehearsal and performance of holiday music: Philosophical issues in *Stratechuk v. Board of Education. Philosophy of Music Education Review, 24*(2), 131–150. https://doi.org/10.2979/philmusieducrevi.24.2.02

Perrine, W. M. (2017a). *Bauchman v. West High School* revisited: Religious text and context in music education. *Philosophy of Music Education Review, 25*(2), 192–213. https://doi.org/10.2979/philmusieducrevi.25.2.06

Perrine, W. M. (2017b). The perils of repressive tolerance in music education curriculum. *Action, Criticism, and Theory for Music Education, 16*(2), 6–38. https://doi.org/10.22176/act16.2.6

Perrine, W. M. (2018). Proselytization and popular music: A policy framework for religious musical expression in public schools. *Arts Education Policy Review, 119*(4), 194–203. https://doi.org/10.1080/10632913.2017.1287800

Pinkney, B. (2005). *Hush, little baby.* New York: HarperCollins.

Playing For Change. (2020). About us: The jorney. https://playingforchange.com

Popkewitz, T. S. (1980). Global education as a slogan system. *Curriculum Inquiry, 10*(3), 303–316.

Popkewitz, T. (2010). The limits of teacher education reforms: School subjects, alchemies, and an alternative possibility. *Journal of Teacher Education, 61*(5), 413–421.

Rankine, A., & Callow, J. (2017). "It's all lighted up, because this is a happy ending": Beginning critical literacy—young children's responses when reading image and text. *Scan, 36*(4), 46–54.

Rappaport, D., & Evans S. W. (2006). *Free at last! Stories and songs of emancipation.* Somerville, MA: Candlewick.

Raschka, C. (1997). *Charlie Parker played be bop.* New York: Scholastic.

Raschka, C. (2002). *John Coltrane's Giant Steps.* New York: Atheneum/Richard Jackson.

ReadWriteThink. (2020). Anticipation guide. http://www.readwritethink.org/classroom-resources/printouts/anticipation-guide-30578.html

Rim, C. (June 4, 2020). How Student Activism Shaped the Black Lives Matter Movement. *Forbes.* Retrieved from https://www.forbes.com/sites/christopherrim/2020/06/04/how-student-activism-shaped-the-black-lives-matter-movement/#1fc05ba74414

Rosenthal, R., & Flacks, R. (2011). *Playing for change: Music and musicians in the service of social movements.* Boulder, CO: Paradigm.

Sachs, J. (2003). *The activist teaching profession.* Buckingham, UK: Open University Press.

Sara. (2008). *Revolución.* Chennai, India: Tara.

Scanlon, T. M. (2003). *The difficulty of tolerance: Essays in political philosophy.* Cambridge: Cambridge University Press.

Schafer, R. M. (1992). *A sound education.* Indian River, ON: Arcana.

Schmidt, P. (2017). Why policy matters: Developing a policy vocabulary within music education. In P. Schmidt & R. Colwell (Eds.), *Policy and the political life of music education* (pp. 11–36). New York: Oxford University Press.

Schmidt, P. (2019). *Policy as practice: A guide for music educators.* New York: Oxford University Press.

Schwadron, A. (1970). On religion, music, and education. *Journal of Research in Music Education, 18*(2), 157–166. https://doi.org/10.2307/3344268

Serafini, F. (2015). Multimodal literacy: From theories to practices. *Language Arts, 92*(6), 412–423.

Shange, N., & Nelson, K. (2004). *Ellington was not a street.* New York: Simon & Schuster Books for Young Readers.

Shankman, E., & O'Neill, E. (2011). *The Bourbon Street band is back.* Beverly, MA: Commonwealth.

Sheff, David. (1981). *All we are saying: The last major interview with John Lennon and Yoko Ono* (G. Barry, Ed., 2000 ed.). New York: St. Martin's Griffin.

Shieh, E. (2018). From below, on the ground, and underneath: Learning policymaking in schools. In M. Chen, A. De Villiers, & A. Kertz- Welzel (Eds.), *Proceedings of the 19th international seminar of the ISME commission on music policy: Culture, education, and media* (pp. 201–215). Munich: International Society for Music Education.

Sirek, D. (2019). Grenadian Music. https://grenadamusic.weebly.com/cultural-context.html

Sleeter, C. (2000). Diversity vs. white privilege. *Rethinking Schools Online, 15*(2), 6.

Stone, S. (1968). Everyday People. [Recorded by Sly and the Family Stone]. As a single. [7" Record]. San Francisco, CA: Pacific High Recording Studios.

Stone, C. (2006). "My beliefs are in my song": Engaging black politics through popular music. *OAH Magazine of History, 20*(5), 28–32. https://doi.org/10.1093/maghis/20.5.28

Street, J. (2012). *Music and politics*. Cambridge, UK: Polity.

Street, J. (2017). Music as political communication. In K. Kenski, K. Jamieson, & J. Street (Eds.), *The Oxford Handbook of Political Communication*. https://doi.org/10.1093/oxfordhb/9780199793471.013.75

Tate, N. (2017). *The conservative case for education: Against the current*. New York: Routledge.

TeachThought: We Grow Teachers. (February 26, 2018). *A Giant List of Really Good Essential Questions*. Retrieved from https://www.teachthought.com/pedagogy/examples-of-essential-questions

Templeton, S. (Director). (2006). *Peter and the wolf* (animated movie). London: Break Thru Films.

Tripp, P., & Gunzenhauser, S. (2006). *Tubby the Tuba*. New York: Dutton Children's Books.

Tripp, P., & Kleinsinger, G. (1948). *The tale of Tubby the Tuba*. Vanguard.

Truax, B. (2001). *Acoustic communication*. Westport, CT: Ablex.

Truth and Reconciliation Commission of Canada. (2015). *Honouring the truth, reconciling for the future: Summary of the final report of the Truth and Reconciliation Commission of Canada*. Winnipeg: Truth and Reconciliation Commission of Canada.

UNESCO. (n.d.a). Core concepts. https://en.unesco.org/interculturaldialogue/core-concepts

UNESCO. (n.d.b). Intercultural dialogue. https://en.unesco.org/themes/intercultural-dialogue

Valenzuela, A. (1999). *Subtractive schooling: U.S.-Mexican youth and the politics of caring*. Albany: State University of New York Press.

Vansieleghem, N. (2005). Philosophy for children as the wind of thinking. *Journal of Philosophy of Education, 39*(1), 19–35. https://doi.org/10.1111/j.0309-8249.2005.t01-1-00417.x

Waks, L. (2011). John Dewey on listening and friendship in school and society. *Educational Theory, 61*(2), 191–205. https://doi.org/10.1111/j.1741-5446.2011.00399.x

Weatherford, C. B. (2000). *The sound that jazz makes*. London: Walker Children's Books.

Wheeler, L., & Christie, R. G. (2007). *Jazz baby*. New York: Houghton Mifflin Harcourt.

Wilson, B. (2014). Teach the how: Critical lenses and critical literacy. *English Journal, 103*(4), 68–75.

Woodford, P. (2014). The eclipse of the public: A response to David Elliott's "Music education as/for artistic citizenship." *Philosophy of Music Education Review, 22*(1), 22–37. https://doi.org/10.2979/philmusieducrevi.22.1.22

Index